"To Build A House"

My surprisingly epic saga in custom home building

By Ryan Haag

To Build A House: My surprisingly epic saga in custom home building by Ryan Haag

Published by Snowy Owl Publishing

www.snowyowlpublishing.org

Cover by Shalone Cason.

www.sdcason.com

Special thanks to my many friends that provided editing support as I built this book.

ISBN: 978-1-7377536-0-5 (print)

Library of Congress Control Number: 2021916461

First Edition

A note and disclaimer to the reader

Thank you for buying this book! Before you delve into the exciting world of my custom house adventure, I need to read you some disclaimers. If I don't, the lawyer said awful things might happen to me, and I certainly don't need that in my life!

This book is written from my point of view about the process of building a custom house from scratch on a virgin piece of land using a loan through the Department of Veterans Affairs program. It's my story. The details are as I remember them. I'm representing my point of view only. Although I was on active duty as a U.S. Navy Officer during that time, nothing in this book represents the views of the U.S. Navy, Department of Defense, or any other government agency.

This book reflects my recollections of the events. I've tried to be as accurate as possible by going through emails, phone logs and official mortgage documents to stay true to the actual timeline. I may still have gotten something wrong, but if I did, it's not through any malice or ill intent. Some of the events have been compressed, and some of the dialogue recreated, because it wasn't written down or recorded at the time it happened.

Humans don't act in a vacuum, and when you build a house, there are a lot of moving parts. More than a few times in the book, I vent my frustration about people and their actions, especially where I feel I was treated poorly. I wrote this book after some time had passed, so that I could let go of many negative emotions. However, some people in this book may feel that they are portrayed in a negative way. I have changed people's names and identifying characteristics in this book to protect their identity. I'm sure if you really wanted to, you could dig through enough public records to uncover these people's identities. Please don't. You aren't doing me any favors if you do this.

Although I am a Sailor, I do not swear in this book, although I swear plenty in person. If you are enjoying the audio version, or leave the book sitting around, rest assured you won't have to explain the meaning of various four lettered words to your children. In general, this is a family friendly book, although there are some sad parts of this book, and I do get angry in parts as well.

This book covers a two-year portion of my life, and includes plenty on non-house building information. It's not a how-to guide on building a custom home, but it does have a lot of lessons I learned in the process. This makes it hard to classify the book in any one way. Some of my editors called it a how-to book. Others called it a saga that delves into religious family development. It's all over the place because it's really a book about my life during the time I built a custom house. During that time, the house building process was the center and focus of most of my efforts, but it wasn't everything. I include an appendix that has just the house building lessons learned, in case you just wanted that information distilled in an easy-to-read fashion.

I published this book because it's in the public's best interest to understand how the custom home building process works. I encountered many pitfalls and snares that are simply not covered in other books. My goal is to illuminate this dark area of construction with the hopes that others will not make the same mistakes I did.

I truly hope you enjoy this book! Should you have questions, please don't hesitate to email me.

For Rebecca

Prologue
January 14, 2019

Today was a crummy day. I am the acting senior intelligence officer for Second Fleet, and part of the glory that comes with working at the Navy's newest numbered fleet is getting up early. Like, really early. In this case, it was 4:30 in the morning (or oh-four-thirty for you military types out there). I was on the road by 5 a.m., and planned to arrive at work no later than 5:45. That would give me enough time to login to my computer and then walk to my first 6:00 meeting, with a ten-to-fifteen-minute buffer for traffic.

Did I mention it's Monday? Mondays apparently hate me. Apparently, I slapped Monday across the face, so Monday called in a hit squad to punish me. This Monday's hit squad got me good too, because my drive to work took nearly two hours. There are four aircraft carriers in port, which adds 5,000 sailors per carrier to our traffic pattern. Coupled with a nasty car accident in the High Occupancy Vehicle Lane, and my chances of getting to work on time were destroyed.

That setback was bad enough, and managed to put me behind on every single piece of paper I owed to my boss that day. But worse was the phone call I received from my wife, Rachel. She told me that the closing for our newly constructed house might not happen tomorrow.

Building a new house has been an epic saga, similar to one of those Greek tragedies that has a steady stream of ironies with ultimate horrific results. Think Macbeth murdering people, or Romeo and Juliet dying. Or me desperately needing to close on my mortgage and not burn through more money just to have a place to live.

Just like those heroic figures in an epic saga, I'm not one to simply stand by and let evil win. Instead of fretting, I asked my wife to Facebook Message the City of Chesapeake's Mayor. Yup, Facebook Message an elected official, because that is SOOOO a Millennial thing to do. Hey, it's 2019, so why not. Rachel sent a Facebook message around 3 p.m. By 4 p.m. I was driving home, talking to my builder about obtaining a Certificate of Occupancy (called a CO, and not to be confused with "Cyber Operations" or "Commanding Officer," for, you know, you military types) in order to finally close the mortgage on the house.

My car has this wonderful feature where it reads off text messages to me so that I'm not tempted to check my phone or text while hurtling down the freeway at 65 miles per hour in thousands of pounds of steel and plastic. This feature is desirable because I'm terribly distractible, and I'm fond of robots, so my car's robotic voice reading off my text messages is a bonus. It's a nerd thing, but if it keeps everyone else safe, it's a positive thing. As my car reads a string of text messages, I quickly realize the Mayor is texting my wife and asking for mortgage and builder details. I told the builder I'd call him back, hung up and then called the Mayor.

There I am, stuck in traffic on my way home on a terrible, horrible, so far, no good very bad Monday, talking to the Mayor of the city I plan on living in. Luckily, Mayor West (yup, that's his real name, not to be confused with the fictional Mayor from *Family Guy*) is a great guy, and after I give him the information he needs, he says he would investigate the situation. By the time I returned home, I had dialed into a phone call with the Deputy City Manager, who is working to have a CO issued so that I can close on my house.

But the day hasn't ended. I have a Cub Scout meeting at 6:30 p.m. (1830 for...well, you know by now). I manage to keep a den of eight third-grade Bear Scouts from tearing apart our meeting area. It seems no matter how hard I run them around, I can never fully eliminate their energy. If I could tap 3rd grade energy, I could probably power a small country, or at least southeastern Virginia. Alas, I am not such a brilliant engineer, so instead I will settle for taking the brunt of the energy while I try to keep the den focused on our meeting.

By the time I've returned home, put my three kids to bed, and checked on my wife (who is suffering from a migraine and is lying on our mattress), it's almost 8 p.m. I check my email from my phone, since we (still) don't have internet yet. Lo and behold, there sits an email from the builder with a temporary CO sent to the mortgage company, in the hopes that it is enough to close tomorrow.

I text my Senior Chief, the senior enlisted Sailor that works for me, to tell her the tentatively wonderful news. Perhaps I'm going to finally close on my house and have one less distraction. She is hopeful, and luckily, we had planned for her to run the department in my absence tomorrow. My hopes are fragile though. I've been let down before. The deeply cynical part of me still expects to get hosed in some way tomorrow.

So, at 10:06 p.m., I decide to start writing my story. Or rather, it's the story of my house. How this house came to be. How I designed this house and built it from scratch. How I nearly lost my mind in the process. How everything that could go wrong, went wrong. If that sounds depressing, don't lose heart, because it's also a story of triumph and how I overcame adversity.

It's not a particularly pretty story, with convenient plot arcs, heroic characters, and evil villains. It's real life, where everything is in shades of gray. People aren't easily put into boxes labeled "good" and "evil." The real world is much harder to organize, and this story deals with real people. Frankly, because it's all true, I think it makes it far more interesting than the fake home construction stories you watch on TV.

This book is about how I built my house from scratch, and learned a thing or two about myself in the process.

Chapter 1
June 30, 2016

Every story has a beginning, and this story begins on a hot day in June at the Devil's Hopyard campground in Connecticut. Most people think of Connecticut, and the north-east in general as dreadfully cold. Those people obviously haven't experienced a summer in Connecticut, and June 30 was a nasty, hot, sweaty sort of day.

On that hot day I was out with my oldest daughter Cecilia and son Neil. My wife Rachel was seven months pregnant and in no mood to spend the night camping in a hot tent. She did come out to visit and brought along our youngest daughter Rosalynn, but she left early to beat the heat. Conveniently, she had a baby check-up appointment the next day, and her mother Elizabeth was in the area to help take her to the hospital.

Joining me and my family at the campground was a large portion of my Navy detachment. I was the Officer in Charge of a detachment of 86 Sailors. Over the past few months, my Sailors had been doing great work installing electronic systems aboard US Navy submarines stationed in Groton, Connecticut, as well as Norfolk, Virginia and Kings Bay, Georgia. I am of the belief that when people work hard and produce excellent results, they need to be rewarded, so we designated the 30th of June as "half-way night" in order to celebrate.

In the submarine Navy, half-way night is a celebration when you cross over the half-way point of your deployment. My Sailors were based at Groton, but we didn't deploy together on one submarine. Instead, I sent two to four Sailors underway on different submarines as that submarine's mission required. Since we didn't have a unified deployment schedule, we picked our date half-way through the calendar year as our half-way night, and after celebrating at work, we concluded our celebration with a picnic and camping trip.

I had warned my Sailors in advance that while I was fine with alcohol at the event, if I caught any underage drinking or dangerous drunkenness, I would put a quick end to the celebration. As the detachment's Officer in Charge, I held non-judicial punishment authority over my Sailors. For those not familiar with the military, this means I can punish small offenses directly, acting as sort of a judge and jury. Luckily, my Sailors didn't want to lose their pay or rank, and while everyone had fun, nobody got out of hand. Good behavior helped me be able to relax, drink and chat with my Sailors around a campfire.

Half-way night was a huge success. Unfortunately, I'm an early riser even when I want to sleep in, so in the morning I woke up, broke down our tent and started driving home with my two oldest kids. On the way back, I saw a traditional looking country diner, so I pulled off the road and we headed in for a much-needed meal. I figured I had lots of time, as my only objective that day was to get home, clean up my camping gear, take a shower and then take a nice long nap. In the diner, my kids and I were dirty, smelly, and thoroughly enjoying our hearty breakfast when my phone rang. It was Rachel.

Rachel: Hey babe.

Me: Hey sweetie! We're almost home, and the kids and I are loving us some pancakes. Let me send you a photo…

Rachel: (interrupting me) You need to turn around.

Me: (With a mouthful of pancake) Huh? I gotta get home and drop off camping gear.

Rachel: Baby has to come today. It's not good.

Me: (Spitting out my pancake) What? What do you mean?

Rachel then explained that during her ultrasound, the doctor saw that the protective amniotic fluid around our baby had suddenly disappeared. He was extremely worried that the baby could die before maturity. A few months back, the ultrasound tech had found a heart defect, so we had been transferred from military treatment to the Yale Hospital. Yes, that Yale Hospital, the really nice one that is a top-of-the-line sort of place. I wasn't going to argue with a Yale doctor. It's *Yale* for crying out loud.

I quickly flagged down the waitress to get my check, confirmed where I had to go, and then paid and left. The kids and I jumped into the vehicle, and faced a terrible problem. Not that I was dirty, smelly, and slightly dehydrated from a night of drinking. Nope, I could deal with all those things.

My problem was that Rachel and I hadn't picked a name for our daughter.

My wife and I are particularly opinionated about naming our children. Or rather, she's opinionated, and just doesn't appreciate the wonderful ideas I have for children's names. It literally takes us months to come to agreement on a kid's name, and it's all because she is an obstinate woman that doesn't understand my great choice in names. I would tease her that since I was the one that filled out the paperwork after birth, it really was solely up to me what our children were named. Rachel would casually remind me that she cooked my meals and that my life insurance was awfully generous should I succumb to a tragic "food poisoning" accident. Since that brings us to a draw, we would fight it out, making fun of each other's name choices while Rachel's belly got bigger.

We hadn't factored in an early baby. So, while I was driving to Yale (about an hour away), I started bouncing names off of Cecilia and Neil.

Me: What about Margaret?

Cecilia: What's the nickname?

Me: Peg or Peggy.

Cecilia: Mmmm, no.

Neil: How about Bernadette?

Me: No way, then she'd be "Bernie" as a girl. She'd be forever picked on as a child and I'd be a terrible excuse for a father.

On and on we tossed names, until...

Me: What about Rebecca? That's a Biblical name, and Rebecca is a pretty strong woman in the Bible.

Cecilia: I like it.

Neil: I like it too.

So "Rebecca" it was. I stopped briefly for gas. When I peeked in the back seat, I noticed both Cecilia and Neil had worried looks on their faces. They knew that something was wrong. Rachel had told me there was a real chance of losing Rebecca at birth, and somehow the kids knew that too. I had to do something, so when we started driving again, I turned on Pandora to our "kids" station, which has mostly Disney, Big Band and other kid friendly music genres. The first song was a blah, but the second was "Love is an open door" from the movie Frozen. My daughter cannot resist singing along, and so the two of us sang along as Anna and Hans as we barreled down I-95 and broke out of our negative moods.

We pulled up to the hospital and met my mother-in-law and Rosalynn. Poor Rosalynn was only four years old and was completely distressed, curled up into a ball in Elizabeth's arms. I handed the kids and car seats to Elizabeth and rushed into the hospital. Rachel was being prepped for a C-section. She was pretty nervous, so I broke the silence by telling her about our name choice. Thankfully, she approved, and my risk of an accidental death early in my life plummeted dramatically.

Rachel had never had a C-section before. Our three previous kids had come out the old-fashioned way, and that actually worked out well for everyone. Rachel was back up and walking within a day after delivery, and by day three in the hospital was clawing at the walls for me to bring her home. No long recovery, no avoiding flights of stairs or other abdominal muscle usage. After our first child was delivered, our second and third child deliveries were not nearly as scary, and we fortunately had almost no complications.

Today was different. I walked into the operating room, and the medical team put up a massive curtain so that all I could see was Rachel's head and upper body. The doctor told me my job was to keep Rachel calm and awake. I nodded my head. Secretly, I was praying that somehow, I didn't pass out. I was dehydrated, dirty, tired and rattled, but luckily Rachel was too doped up to notice.

I managed to stay coherent through the procedure. Oh, and Rachel did great, just in case you were wondering. While the procedure went smoothly, baby Rebecca was not in good shape. She was rushed into the NICU. After I helped wheel Rachel to her recovery room, I headed to the NICU to find her, where I was told I'd have to wait.

Let me tell you what sucks: waiting. Waiting outside a NICU sucks. There are pictures at Yale's NICU showing all the really hard-case babies that the NICU saved. One kid was only 1 pound when he was born and had to have chemo-therapy, and yet he lived. That's pretty amazing! What isn't shown are all the kids that didn't make it. I've visited enough cemeteries to understand that newborn death is a distinct possibility, and waiting outside the NICU only amplified this worry.

To pass the time, I blearily paced the halls. When I finally got back to see Rebecca, she was on a ventilator. Her oxygen saturation stats were low, likely due to her heart defect. I asked the doctor what her chance of success was, and he wouldn't give me a straight answer, which I interpreted as "not good." Not knowing what else to do, I sat at Rebecca's side and prayed a rosary.

When I was done, I prayed another one. I couldn't think of what to do next...and then it hit me. Rebecca might not survive today, and she needed to be baptized. I'm Roman Catholic, so Baptism is kind of a big deal, since it saves you from the grip of Original Sin. I called the local parish and asked for an emergency baptism. A priest rushed to the NICU, and a hospital administrator let Rachel be wheeled in so she could see Rebecca. I made sure to record it on my phone, since Rachel looked a bit drugged and would likely not remember this moment. Since Rebecca was stuck in a NICU bed and hooked onto a ventilator, the priest had to use a small bottle of holy water and dab it on her forehead.

I stayed in the NICU for a while longer, then saw Rachel to bed and drearily walked to my car. I drove home that day exhausted, still dirty and now depressed. After a shower at home, I sat on the couch with my kids in near silence. Rebecca might not survive the night. It wasn't the delivery experience I was expecting.

Poor little Rebecca struggled over the next two days. She was the largest baby in the NICU, but her weight couldn't stop her whole body from shaking with every puff of the ventilator. She couldn't cry because of the tube sticking all the way down her throat. Most of the time, we couldn't even touch her, and certainly not hold her. My wife and I were stuck observing her through clear plastic casing, as if she was an exotic aquarium fish. She stared back at us, wondering why she was going through such pain.

Two days later, Rebecca was still clinging to life when a team of doctors called us into a room to discuss something. I was really nervous, because I figured this is where we got the "your child is not going to live" speech and had to discuss how long she could stay on a ventilator. I had watched people die before, and during my Naval Service I'd helped kill more than a few bad apples in the world. But it's different when it's your own kid. It's downright scary, and I was particularly scared as we sat down on a couch with the doctor.

Doctor: Mr. and Mrs. Haag, I have some news to share with you.

Me: (In a slow, nervous voice) Go on...

Doctor: The genetic testing came back, and your daughter has Down Syndrome.

Me: Uhm....

Yes, I was speechless, because at the time, I had no clue what Down Syndrome was. What's sad is that had the doctor stated that Rebecca had Trisomy-21, I would have understood what that meant, as I have a science background. Rachel and I sat in this closet of an office asking question after question, but on the inside, we were just numb.

Down Syndrome happens when someone has three chromosomes in the 21st pair of chromosomes. That's why the technical name for it is Trisomy-21. Most trisomy genetic disorders result in miscarriage, but Trisomy-21 has a higher chance of live birth. All of my Google research indicated that of all the trisomy disorders, Down Syndrome was the one with the highest chance for survival. It wasn't going to be easy though, because that extra chromosome had some pretty drastic effects, including mental impacts, low muscle tone and speech impairment.

Over the next few days, I learned more about Down Syndrome. I read lots of loving stories about people raising kids with Down Syndrome. There were whole groups devoted to raising money to helping Down Syndrome kids. I even found out that adults with Down Syndrome were eligible for federal money in the event they couldn't work. My Googling was getting pretty positive at this point.

Then cold hard reality hit again. There is a funny tendency with internet searches to self-select for the stories you want, and in my case that was positive stories. When I began asking the doctors at Yale about raising kids with Down

Syndrome, I got some more sober answers. Most of the nurses described the negative side effects: low muscle tone, poor coordination, speech problems and mental struggles. One nurse talked about how Down's kids would get picked on relentlessly in school. And for one doctor, his advice was pretty clear: "It's nice to think things will be normal, but you should be prepared to have a permanent child at home."

That comment dropped on me like a ton of bricks. For my entire life, I hadn't lived in one spot for more than three years. My dad was a Marine Corps officer and retired right before I left for college. In college, I had moved every year, sometimes twice a year. After college, I joined the Navy and then moved so much that I averaged one and a half moves a year! At this point, I had taken my wife and family to Virginia, California, Georgia, Hawaii and Connecticut in a span of less than ten years.

Rachel and I had discussed building our "forever home" at some point in the future. For the non-military types reading this book, a military "forever home" is that dream house you buy when you get out of the military. It's in the perfect neighborhood, with great schools for your kids, and the best part is you don't have to leave it after three years. No more moving boxes. No more movers breaking all your stuff and offering you ten percent of its actual replacement value. No more leaving your friends. No more crying kids as you drive away from the neighborhood leaving behind the school friends they grew to love. None of that.

It's your house, permanently, exactly how you want it.

As a military member, you yearn for forever home. When I was in SERE school, which stands for Survival, Evasion, Resistance and Escape, we were taught how to evade an enemy and then, when captured, how to resist interrogation. One of the tricks to combating the long periods of quiet was to design your forever home in your head. Man, I designed my house over and over again while sitting in a hot jail cell in Warner Springs, California. My forever home was perfect, and made me smile while my interrogator smacked me around like a bad side of tuna.

Rachel had also designed forever home in her head, over and over again. Our constant moving gave us the advantage of living in different types of housing layouts. Open concept? Done that. Basement? Lived with one too. Laundry in the upstairs, downstairs and basement? Guest bedroom and no guest bedroom? Yup, lived with all that and more. These experiences gave us a solid understanding of what we wanted and what we didn't want in forever home.

But forever home just sits in your head. When the military issues you another set of orders, after the initial excitement abates, depression sets in again, because you realize you kicked forever home down the road a few more years. When it became apparent that I would stay in the Navy for at least twenty years, forever home wasn't coming until

2024, which seems like it'll never happen. Forever home was just a dream.

Until now. Suddenly forever home was extraordinarily real, because Rebecca would need a forever home. But first, Rebecca had to survive the NICU. And that journey wasn't going to be easy.

Chapter 3
July 10, 2016

Being in the NICU sucks. The NICU is the Neonatal Intensive Care Unit. It's designed to take care of babies that need intensive care. Yale has one of the best NICUs in the country, and probably the world. The doctors and nurses at Yale's NICU are top notch professionals that have done cutting edge research and medical care. Treat babies for cancer at only twenty-four weeks old? Conduct heart surgery on a two-pound baby? Most hospitals call that impossible, but at Yale, the doctors simply call it Tuesday, work their magic and move on with their day.

None of that bravado makes staying in the NICU easy. The actual NICU area is designed to administer medical care, with no eye towards comfort. Not surprisingly, it is not comfortable to sit there. As the parent of a child clinging to life on a ventilator, you might imagine I would be in there every single minute of every day. For the first two days, I sure felt like I was. But soon after that, it became...well, boring. I wasn't allowed to hold Rebecca, so we couldn't just sit and bond. Instead, I got to stare at her through a plastic screen, like a fish at an aquarium. Let me tell you, I already find aquariums somewhat boring, and watching a little baby do essentially nothing is boring too.

That might sound harsh. You might think "What an insensitive jerk!" And at first, I thought the same thing of myself. I would walk back to Rachel's recovery room thinking I was a terrible human being for being bored while my child navigated the razor's edge of survival. Rachel felt the same way. The first few days, she tried to spend every waking minute in the NICU, but it soon grew boring. Sure, she could pump some breast milk for the nurses to feed Rebecca with, but that took only forty-five minutes a day, tops. The rest of the time, she was watching the aquarium.

We did have a looming quandary on our minds, because we had to figure out where to stay. I had sent our kids to my parent's house for a month, since we expected Rebecca to have some NICU time. We had initially thought we would commute to and from our home in Groton to visit Rebecca. This was an hour-long drive one-way, and with no end in sight for the NICU, it wasn't sustainable. Worse still, Yale did not have a Ronald McDonald house at that time, because it was undergoing significant renovations. What could we do instead? Well, in our case, we got lucky. Rachel's parents graciously offered to pay for us to stay in a nearby medical hotel. The hotel provided free transportation to and from Yale, which was important since Rachel couldn't walk well the first week after a C-section. It gave us the ability to visit Rebecca multiple times a day while also being able to leave and relax nearby.

Another problem soon emerged: how in the heck were we going to eat? I had assumed we'd be eating out for only a week. Meals in Hartford are expensive, even in the summer without college students. Luckily, I got bailed out once again. At my Navy command, we have a volunteer position called an Ombudsman, who is the family member of a Sailor that helps Navy families integrate into Navy life. Her name was Lezlie Gingerich, and while I had only known her for about a month at this point, we quickly built a great working relationship. Lezlie signed us up for a Meal Train, which is a website where people can purchase meals for families in need. The nice thing is the meals are deconflicted by day, so you don't get thirty orders of Chick-Fil-A all on one day from your well-meaning friends.

Lezlie's meal train saved our sanity. She shared the link on social media, and soon our friends were filling our days with hot meals from local restaurants. The constant back and forth between the hospital, the lack of knowledge on whether Rebecca would live, or even when she would leave the NICU, added stress to our lives. That stress made it hard to do simple things such as cook a basic meal. Coming back from a long day and finding a meal delivered to our door made the world, for that brief instance, a slightly better place for us. I'm forever indebted to my family and friends that purchased a meal for us on the Meal Train when we were most in need. If you're reading this book right now, thank you.

The nurses at Yale became our other saviors. I would strike up conversations with the various NICU nurses, and it didn't take long to find common ground. Before long I was listening to stories about medical school while I shared the PG-13 rated sea stories from my past. We bonded

Chapter 4
July 21, 2016

When most people think about building a custom home, they imagine the fun things such as picking out wall colors, granite slabs and kitchen layouts. In their dreams they imagine walking around a custom house in their pajamas, gleefully tapping in empty space to make a kitchen island, under-cabinet lighting, jetted tubs and heated towel racks magically appear out of thin air. Admit it, you probably had that daydream too. It's OK, everyone has to grow up at some point.

As a cynical Navy officer, much of my vocabulary is built on words that start with the letter 'F'. As I sank into my grinding routine at the hospital, this didn't change much. I was planning out "forever home," and my first thoughts concerned foundations, floor plans and functions. Lots of 'F' words all the time, so much that I would get the occasional eye roll from my wife when I excitedly discussed encapsulated crawl spaces (more on that point later!).

First though, we should talk about the definition of a "custom home." When you buy an existing home, you buy a house that you can move into the next day. You get its current charm and charisma, floor plan and most furnishings, but you also get its flaws. Walls poorly insulated and color not to your liking? Guess what, you're stuck with it. You can renovate it, but a lot of basics, such as load bearing walls and foundation type, are hard if not impossible to change without a lot of money. If you watch home renovation shows on TV, you may think this easy, and you would be correct, if you have a team of well-paid professionals at your beckon call to tear apart and rebuild rooms at the snap of your fingers. Since most people don't have this sort of support in their hip pocket, you'll either pay a lot of money or do much of the work yourself, with plenty of four lettered words to accompany you when things become difficult.

If you buy a house in a large neighborhood under construction, and let's say the house is almost done, you might get to customize the granite and wall colors. If you had gotten there earlier, you could pick from one of several floorplan options, all with their increasing price points. That sounds similar to a custom house, but really it should be called a "some custom options house." You don't get to change the foundation or other critical elements of the house with the builder.

I wanted my own house, laid out how I wanted, with features I picked. That's custom to me. Because my Navy career required moving every two to three years, I have lived in a variety of floorplans and dealt with more home maintenance issues than I care to admit. I wanted to start at the ground level and build something that wouldn't have the flaws I had lived in throughout my Navy career. It's similar getting the perfect start on a computer game that makes the follow-on missions more fun. Nobody enjoys playing a computer game with a character that rolled poor stats.

I had to educate myself, and with time on my hands, I did what any Millennial would do (or Xenial, or whatever silly classification I belong in for being born in the early '80s), and I watched a lot of YouTube. I soon became a huge fan of Matt Risinger, who is a builder that really cares about building science. I'm an engineer, and I love science, so Matt Risinger's discussions about how to build correctly was right up my alley.

Matt, if you're reading this book, I'm totally your biggest fan.

Anyway, one of the first key points about a house is the foundation. It's the thing that the entire house rests on, so it's kind of a big deal. Since it's that big of a deal, it was worth watching every Matt Risinger video about foundations. Foundations can be confusing because you can pick from a few options. In Virginia, most homes are built on slab foundations. First, the builder digs down a certain number of feet and puts in some forms. Then he pours concrete into these forms to make footers. The footers are where the weight of the house gets pushed into the soil. These footers have a larger surface area on the bottom (the part that touches the soil) and a smaller area on top, so the weight gets disbursed over a lot of soil. Imagine a bunch of pyramids sunk into the ground, with the house's weight pushing on the tips. As that force of the house's weight travels down the pyramids, it gets spread over a larger surface area, and the ground below it pushes up and thus holds up your house.

Above the footers sits the foundation. In the case of a slab, its, well, a humongous slab of concrete. There are some pipes buried in the slab so that electrical and plumbing lines can be run under the house. This causes problems later on because if a water pipe breaks, you have to jack hammer the pipes out of the slab, then repour the concrete, all while making sure the house doesn't put too much weight on that part of the foundation. Not a fun task, and not one I particularly wanted. So, no slab foundation for me.

On the other end of the foundation spectrum is a basement, where you dig deeper for the footers, put a slab in and then build up walls that are below the soil level. The pipes and electrical wires are all in the basement ceiling, and it's easy to run new wires or repair old ones since you can reach everything. But you have to keep a basement dry, and in coastal Virginia, that's a bit of a problem due to a high-water table and lots of rain from hurricanes. So, basements were out of the picture.

The sweet spot in the middle is a crawl space. On top of the concrete footers are concrete blocks. These blocks create a low space that you can crawl into, hence the name crawl space. The crawl space gives you access to pipes and wiring under your house, without being deep enough to bring up significant ground water. Unfortunately, most crawl spaces are a bit nasty, featuring wonderful residents such as spiders, raccoons and mold. Imagine yourself in a horror movie where you're in a cramped space, except you can't move fast enough and a monster drags you into the depths of your dark, dirty, nasty crawl space. Yuck! Not a movie I wanted to see.

One of the Matt Risinger videos I watched talked about a conditioned crawl space. The "conditioned" part means you put a thick tarp on the ground, insulate the sides, and install a dehumidifier to keep the space dry. Now you have the best of all worlds: your house is up, you can work on pipes, you have no critters underneath, and you don't have to worry about keeping a full basement dry. Best of all, there is no abominable horror movie to watch. I wanted a conditioned crawl space.

While I worked on picking my home's foundation, I also worked on building my relationship foundation with my wife. Rachel and I had been through plenty of rough times before. We had moved from Virginia to California, then to Virginia, then Georgia, then Hawaii and then to Connecticut, all in the span of eight years. During that time, I had deployed overseas twice, traveled on multiple smaller trips, and spent months in between moves at various schools. So, despite being married for almost ten years, we hadn't spent all that much time together.

Living at the hospital and doing the same thing, day in and day out was exhausting. I had to dig deep to encourage Rachel with small steps. Any lady listening that has had a C-section knows how much it sucks to slowly regain your ability to walk any sort of distance afterwards. This was made worse by the fact that all our previous babies had been natural deliveries, and Rachel had been home and moving around the next day. Now we were at the mercy of the hospital transport people.

Over the next month, we slowly progressed from requiring transport, to walking around the apartment, to walking down the street, to walking one-way to visit Rebecca, and eventually to walking there and back twice a day. Every little bit of progress pushed her closer to normal. Every bit of progress made us grow as a couple.

Rebecca made progress too. First it was getting her oxygen saturation levels up. I would sit there and pray over her, staring at the oxygen meter, willing the number to go up. Slowly this happened. First the supplemental oxygen level she needed dropped to nothing, and eventually the nurses removed those bottles. Then her oxygen saturation stayed above ninety percent, and the nurses removed the ventilator. Now we could actually see her face and she could cry normally. She still slept most of the time, but it was a huge improvement.

Eventually, after three weeks, we were allowed to hold her. Not super independently mind you. Rebecca still had lots of wires hooked up. I smiled as I watched her oxygen levels spike high the first time Rebecca nuzzled next to Rachel. It was a beautiful sight to behold. Our family was finally getting pieced back together.

Chapter 5

August 2, 2016

While Rachel's day job was visiting Rebecca, pumping breast milk and trying to stay positive, as our NICU stay crested over three weeks I began to realize I would soon run out of leave days unless I returned to work. As the Officer in Charge of a detachment of 86 sailors, I couldn't just not be there. I had done a decent job staying on top of some work via my personal computer, but too much of what I did required access to a classified computer that I would have to use in my secure office.

In the NICU there is no sense of time and doctors have no urgent reason to release you. This is understandable given the fragile condition of its residents. Finally, after a long day spent going back and forth to Yale, I sat down with Rachel and talked about our options. We agreed that I had to go back home, but that it made sense for her to stay here, at least a little while longer.

So, on a hot August day, I headed back to my house in Ledyard, Connecticut, just outside of Groton. It was only a one-hour drive, but leaving my wife and baby behind, especially with Rebecca's still yet to be determined fate, really sucked. My house was empty, since my kids were still at my mom and dad's house on a "summer break," which was really a "I want you far away in case Rebecca doesn't make it" visit. My first day back at work was a lot of "bleh." Catching up on email and being briefed on all the things I missed made it hard to physically leave my office to see my Sailors, which was always the high point of my day. I had a car appointment in the afternoon, so I left early to complete the oil change, tire rotation and all that other car maintenance I had been ignoring the past few weeks.

I nearly fell asleep at the dealership. I figured it was fatigue from returning to work. I drove home, not really feeling well at all. My house was dark, so I fumbled around, found the light and made myself a simple meal. I sat on the couch to watch some YouTube...and felt worse. Then I realized I was hot. No, not because I had an impeccable beach body. I touched my head and it was physically really hot. I started drinking water. Soon I realized I couldn't drink enough water to bring my temperature down. Crap. I headed to my car to drive to the hospital, then realized I couldn't see straight. I was in trouble. I called 911.

The ambulance arrived at my house, loaded me up, and off to the New London Hospital we traveled. I called my Duty Officer to tell him I was headed to the hospital, since it was his job to track whenever my Sailors had significant medical issues, even if that Sailor was me. Arriving at the hospital, I was hooked up to an IV, then I fell asleep, exhausted.

I woke up to a familiar voice. "Hey sir, kinda odd we should meet like this." Opening my eyes, I realized it was my new Assistant Officer in Charge, Josh Robishaw. He had reported to the command while I was at the NICU, but we had met each other before at a previous duty station in Georgia. I smiled at Josh and sighed "Yeah, I guess this counts as your check-in huh." We both had a chuckle, and the nurse stopped by to check on me. Ultimately, she couldn't find anything wrong with me, but at least the IV seemed to help. Maybe it was too much stress? I never figured it out. The nurse did check Josh out, and she was cute, and when she walked out, I nudged Josh and whispered "You should get her number." Josh, being the gentleman, did not get her number, and instead he drove me home that night. I felt like a terrible wingman as I slowly climbed the stairs and drifted into much-needed sleep. Two days later, I was back at the office without a problem.

It's weird being in a quiet house. I had grown accustomed to the constant noise from three children, who ran upstairs and downstairs, scattering toys in various rooms between the complaints of being bored. Every parent of multiple children understands these frustrations. It was these challenges that made me think about the number and types of rooms I wanted in our forever home.

The idea of an "open concept" house is really popular. It means that instead of doors or narrow passageways between rooms, you have open spaces that sort of "flow" into each other. The open concept makes it easy to move between rooms, host larger parties, and be an inviting place for everyone. Everyone likes an open concept house, and I mean everyone. If you watch one of those home shows on television, eventually someone is knocking out a wall with a sledge hammer while yammering on about "impeding flow" or "impounding chi" or some other hippy idea. The cult of open concept housing is alive and well in America, at least in 2016.

But in Hawaii, I had a house with an open concept, and it was horrible. The living room, dining room and kitchen were all one vast room in a straight line. This meant that any noise in these rooms radiated quickly between all the rooms. With three kids, there was a lot of noise. And boy did it radiate! My wife would be cooking in the kitchen and would constantly yell at our kids to go outside. Now, this was Hawaii, so going outside every day is totally doable. But forever home wouldn't be in Hawaii. We needed a better plan.

We had a neighbor across the street in Hawaii that had a similar house design, but with one key difference. Instead of one straight room, the three rooms were arranged in an "L" shape, with the kitchen at the corner of the "L" and the living room and dining room on different branches. This bend made it harder for sound to travel, and it broke up the room in a nicer-looking shape. I really liked that design. However, in Groton our house's first floor had rooms that opened in a circle, which encouraged kids to run in circles with no end in sight. It resembled a track, or a circus, and it certainly felt that way when streams of kids would run laps inside. I bought into the cult of the open concept floor plan, but I picked the "L" shaped Kool-Aid flavor, because I think it's the best flavor.

I also decided on five bedrooms, which included a downstairs bedroom guest suite. That left a bedroom for girls, one for boys, and one as a nursery. I had spent considerable time the past few weeks reading about the challenges for kids with Down Syndrome. Most children with Down Syndrome lacked normal muscle tone which made it hard to play, attend school and simply be a normal kid. It might be a while before Rebecca could move out, and perhaps she might never move out of our home. I wanted to have enough rooms that this wouldn't cause problems for my other kids.

The guest suite was a must have, which sounds weird unless you are in the military. I was not going to settle down near my family nor Rachel's family. That meant that family would travel to visit us, and once you grow beyond a certain age, crashing on someone's couch is not exactly the best sign of hospitality. Rachel and I wanted our parents to be able to visit for extended periods of time and be comfortable. Even better, since Norfolk was a common place for my military friends to travel through, a guest suite made it easy to host them for a night of good food, good beer and good sea stories.

I was also concerned about aging parents. I was in my thirties, and both Rachel's parents and mine were getting older. As the oldest of three boys, I felt it was my responsibility to take care of my parents if they became sick. I had watched a friend pay thousands of dollars every month to a nursing home taking care of his dad. It drained him financially, physically, mentally and spiritually. I could see the lines on his face and long stare whenever I brought the subject up. In the end, the nursing home drained his father's savings account, and after he died, there was little in his apartment left to clean up. I remember the bitterness in his voice when we drove back after gathering his dad's remaining stuff from that nursing home. I did not desire that fate for my parents or Rachel's parents.

After another week, Rachel was beginning to get restless. Her whole life had been wrapped up in being a wife and a mother, but at the NICU, where our incredibly kind nurses did most of the work, Rachel was now spending a lot of time sitting around. It was wearing on her soul. I could hear it in her voice whenever we spoke on the phone. After a few long drives back and forth from Groton to Yale, I was beginning to wear down as well. Our kids summer vacation with my parents was nearing an end, and I needed Rachel home to watch them. At this point, Rebecca had been in the NICU for a month. Rebecca's doctors were now talking about when she would go home, not if she would go home. The first time it happened, I took notice. Perhaps our prayers were being answered after all!

Chapter 6
August 8, 2016

I brought Rachel home on August 8th. As we drove from Yale back to Groton, I could tell she was torn. She didn't miss the NICU, but leaving our baby behind was gut wrenching, despite Rebecca staying at possibly the best hospital in the world. I tried to talk to her about the detachment, my Sailors, my work, the kids coming back from my parent's house, anything to brighten her spirits. The blank look on her face told me she was having none of it. I finally accepted defeat and quietly piloted our vehicle home.

I had planned for Rachel to return a few days before my kids came back. This gave her a chance to become re-acquainted with the house and build up a normal schedule. In the military, we call this a battle rhythm. Having a battle rhythm helps maintain a routine that accomplishes tasks, and it guides your Sailors as to what is next. Battle rhythms create routine out of chaos, and prevent insane situations from running amuck. Rachel needed her battle rhythm before our children added chaos to our schedule.

My parents drove my kids back three days later. The next day, we all headed to see Rebecca at Yale. Although still in her fish bowl, we could at least hold her, which made all the difference in the world. Since the NICU is a tight space, the hospital only let in two visitors at a time, so we had to alternate kids and parents back and forth from the waiting room. While waiting, the area outside the NICU had posters of nice-looking kids, with the crazy challenges that the Yale staff had to overcome. One kid had a birth weight of only two pounds and had to undergo cancer treatment shortly after birth, but was pictured at age eight as healthy and wanting to play baseball. Those posters gave me hope that we could make it out of the NICU.

Having my parents over was great, and having the kids back brought some normalcy to our lives. Rachel and I had been living on our own for over a month. It was a bit of a shock getting back into our battle rhythm, and we quickly realized how insufficient our current house was in terms of space for our personal pursuits. It forced us to consider the functionality we needed for forever home, which included an office and a crafting room.

I spend a lot of time at the keyboard. Much of that is for work, but I'm also a big computer gamer. My Ledyard home computer was setup in the "den" of the house, and I would constantly have a small companion (my son) watching me play. Most of the time it was fine, but when I occasionally beheaded a Nord warrior in *Skyrim*, or hacked up a drowner in *The Witcher*, well, my wife did not take kindly to that. An office with a door solves that problem, so it joined our list of requirements.

My wife had a similar issue. No, she wasn't slaying aliens in *XCOM 2*, but she did have a multitude of stamps and crafting things. These stamps are cute and small, which makes them an attractive nuisance for children. If Rachel tried to work on a project, she would have to complete it in one sitting, or else the kids would inevitably walk off with her crafting gear. "Steal" is such a harsh word. Perhaps the phrase "appropriate for play time" is more appropriate? Anyway, similar to my office, a crafting room quickly became a requirement.

As our requirements for forever home grew, we started paying attention to another set of requirements. Rebecca was finally getting better, and the doctors were beginning to talk about what she needed to demonstrate in order to come home. First was eating. One of Down Syndrome's nasty side effects is a lack of muscle tone. Rebecca was tired after even the most basic things. She could breast feed, but not for very long. She would quickly tire and need rest, all the while burning calories that she had to replace. To solve this, the nurses placed a feeding tube down her nose that would deposit food into her stomach. It's called a G-tube, with the "G" standing for gastrointestinal. When she was newly born, the tube wasn't a big deal, but now that Rebecca was a bit older, she developed the unpleasant habit of pulling it out of her nose. In the NICU, this isn't a problem. At home, it would be.

Rachel and I got our first lesson in G-tube placement. The nurses showed us the proper way to feed the tube down the nose and throat and ensure it was deep enough. The tricky part was, if

Rebecca fought the tube going down, it would likely wind up coming out of her mouth. You had to shove a tiny, flexible silicone tube very quickly down a screaming, writhing child's nose without them coughing it up. If that sounds like fun, you should re-examine your life's choices. Or become a NICU nurse, because then you'll be paid for these undesirable activities.

The nurses had me practice first, because picking on the guy that doesn't much care for hospitals, blood or anything related to poking or prodding the human body is apparently a great idea. Yes, I am in fact not a fan of any of those things, and even talking about them makes me squeamish. That's why I'm ecstatic that other people sign up to be nurses. Anyway, I took Rebecca in one hand and the G-tube in the other. I got Rebecca to look at me, and she smiled. She probably just liked the attention, since I have a pretty grisly mug. I smiled back. Then I blanked out my mind and lost all emotions, and I swiftly rammed the tube down Rebecca's little nose. Her shocked face reassured me I had caught her completely by surprise, and luckily, the tube was well down her throat before her gag reflex could try to catch it.

Score one for me. Hopefully my emotions returning and my guilt over savagely shoving a tube down my daughter's throat meant I retained some of my humanity despite the savage process. After some practice, Rachel was able to thread the G-tube to the nurse's satisfaction. We completed step one, huzzah!

Step two was for Rebecca to be off oxygen. The nurses and doctors had been slowly weaning her off, so that she could breathe normal air without losing oxygen saturation in her blood. After forty days in the NICU, the supplemental oxygen was no longer attached to her face, and the bottle was simply sitting nearby for emergency use only. I noticed that every time we held Rebecca, her oxygen saturation level rose dramatically. Rachel and I spent the next several days with lots of skin-to-skin contact time. After enough oxygen saturation spikes, the saturation level stayed high enough and the doctors were satisfied.

But the doctors had more requirements. It seemed the list was endless. The whole time, we watched other kids come into the NICU and then leave. We had a few families that we grew close to. Rebecca's neighbor was a little boy that was only three pounds with many health problems. It helped to have someone to talk to that was in the same crap situation we were. Rachel even offered to donate her extra breast milk to help him out, which the family graciously accepted.

I need to pause here a second to talk about breast milk donation. Plenty of hospitals need breast milk, especially a NICU, where formula is just not a great substitute for breast milk. But if you're thinking of donating, beware! You better not take any medication, smoke, drink alcohol, think bad thoughts, have the smallpox vaccine, swear uncontrollably at work, or have any other vices, or else your milk is automatically inferior and can't be accepted. And even if you think that swearing and medications are valid concerns, medications include pretty much any supplement, including most vitamins. If you're like most people and take supplements to curb cravings or improve your workout, breast milk donation is out of the question, and you either freeze the extra or pour it down the sink with your tears.

Seriously. It's probably easier to give blood than donate breast milk.

Rebecca changed neighbors a lot. Some kids would leave with their parents, and we'd wave to them, only to never see them again. I'd see other kids in desperate shape, and the next day they were gone. I'd ask about them, and the quiet reply from the nurses about protecting privacy information, plus the downward stare at their shoes, would tell me all I needed to know about their fate. As our NICU stay dragged into day forty-five, I was beginning to worry that our fate would be the same.

Chapter 7
August 23, 2016

Our luck changed quickly. Rebecca continued to make progress, and the doctor finally told us it was time to prepare to take her home. Rebecca would require heart surgery to fix an Atrial Septal defect and her tricuspid valve, but that would be much later. If none of those body part names made sense to you, you are not alone. The doctors and surgeons attempted to explain all these problems to Rachel and I using a whiteboard, but it just didn't work. After another confusing session with a doctor, we were walking out of the hospital when I had a bright idea.

"Rachel, we should bring a Giant Microbe Heart Plush next time!"

If you aren't familiar with Giant Microbes, they are plush dolls shaped into viruses, cells, or other biological structures. I first encountered Giant Microbes on a trip to Charlottesville, where I found an Ebola Zaire virus microbe. I always thought the Ebola virus was unique and cool, or at least as cool as a nasty virus that kills over sixty percent of its victims can be from a distance, so that Giant Microbe came home with me. Ever since then, our kids have been hooked on Giant Microbes. The original series had expanded to include organs, and now featured a large, anatomically correct heart. We got one delivered and brought it to our next surgeon meeting, and it made so much sense that the surgeon decided he needed to order them. Did I just bring a spectacular idea to the best hospital in the world? Does that make me an absolute genius? The answer to both of these questions is a resounding yes!

Now to describe the surgery. There are four chambers in the heart, two on top and two on the bottom. A normal heart uses its right side to collect blood with little to no oxygen, then pumps it to the lungs to absorb oxygen, after which that blood comes into the left side of the heart. The left side of the heart then pumps this oxygenated blood to the rest of the body. Rebecca's Atrial Septal defect meant that the top two chambers of the heart had a hole in the wall that was supposed to separate them. This hole meant oxygenated blood and non-oxygenated blood mixed, which caused her to have less oxygenated blood pumped to the rest of her body. But that wasn't Rebecca's only problem. Separating the top and bottom chambers is the tricuspid valve. The tricuspid valve is a three-flap valve that prevents backflow when the heart pumps. Because Rebecca's valve was malformed, she had further problems keeping enough oxygenated blood flowing in her body.

Not enough oxygen made Rebecca extremely lethargic. Combined with the low muscle tone that Down Syndrome brings on, and Rebecca struggled to do all the basic things a baby does: eat, move her head, try to crawl and other baby motions. I would watch her attempt to nurse and quickly become exhausted. Her heart would require surgery, but the doctors wanted her to grow a bit larger so that she had a higher chance of surviving surgery. Suddenly, they wanted to send her home.

Just that suddenly, we were in a rush. We had to setup our G-tube pump, finish the nursery, prep our house, and all that in a few days. We also had to accept that she was actually coming home. You would think that would be easy, that the whole time we were in the hospital we were pining to return home. And we were. But after you've been hanging on for well over a month, you start to think you'll just be stuck forever. And then "BAM," you're prepping to go home, and you feel totally unprepared.

Rachel and I drove to the hospital on day fifty-four of the NICU to bundle up Rebecca and bring her home. We brought our car seat into the hospital and buckled her into it, being careful to not catch her G-tube on any of the buckles. Then off we walked, loaded her in the car, jumped into our seats...and just paused. It felt weird. I looked at Rachel, and we both looked back at Rebecca, who was dozing in the seat. Without another word, we pulled out of the parking garage and onto I-95, taking what was finally a one-way trip home.

The next few weeks were rough. But I had been trained for rough living. At SERE school, the survival school I previously mentioned, you learn how to evade people hunting you, survive in the wild, resist interrogation, and ultimately escape from your captors. I got slapped, starved and stuffed into many a small box, all in the name of training. But the worst part was the sleep deprivation. The camp we stayed in would play music all night of kids screaming, raunchy pop music and the occasional poorly worded propaganda speech. If you thought Miley Cyrus was dreadful, imagine listening to her greatest hits, out of tune and warbled a bit. I still shudder just thinking about it.

SERE school got it wrong though. The absolute worst way to destroy sleep is through medical devices. They are true torture. Rebecca's gavage feeding pump had three unique sounds, and that pump would beep for about twenty-eight different reasons. Is the attached bag out of milk? Did the pump lose priming? Was there a power fluctuation? Is there not enough moonlight? Did the drywall in the house have the wrong fluctuations in its quantum states? Any of these real or imagined reasons would cause the pump to alarm with an incessant and constant beep. Worse, it wasn't the same series of button pushes to make the beeping stop. When you setup a feed at midnight, and then it happily chimes completion at 3 a.m., the pump keeps chiming until you lumber out of bed, walk down the hall, stub your toe on the edge of the door frame, and then bang your fingers mindlessly on a keypad until it stopped yelling at you. Do that for two weeks, and you'll become a zombie quicker than if an actual zombie bit you.

It was at this time that my wife laid down another rule for forever home: upstairs laundry. Most homes in Connecticut had basements, including our home. Our laundry was in the basement. We found out quite quickly that three kids' laundry, plus our own, plus a baby's laundry meant that Rachel lugged laundry up and down two sets of stairs nearly every day. Combined with sleep deprivation, running the laundry circuit everyday gave us a CrossFit workout, except your massive gains are dark circles around your eyes instead of intense muscle tone in your abs. Rachel demanded that our forever home have an upstairs laundry. I was worried about water damage, but after a long stare from Rachel, I discovered plenty of YouTube videos that discussed how to properly waterproof an upstairs laundry room. Since the problem was able to be solved, and I did not desire to fight my zombie wife lest she bite me, I wrote down "upstairs laundry" as another forever home requirement.

Over the next two months we slowly adjusted to life with Rebecca at home. We got constant visits from her therapist, who helped teach Rebecca how to roll over, move her head and compensate for low muscle tone. I made it a chore for my kids to ensure she had "tummy time" every day, which forced her to workout. We talked with other parents of Down Syndrome kids, and the ones that had the smallest number of issues told us that intensive therapy was critical for future success. We made therapy a routine, and things seemed to progress just fine.

With our house design nearly complete, at least in our heads, we needed to figure out where to put down roots. We had settled on the Hampton Roads area of Virginia, but we needed to pick an actual city and school district. I took some much-needed leave, we packed up in a car, and we headed down to Virginia Beach to visit friends and stay at a beach house. During my two weeks off, I must have driven past every major area, from the expansive farms of Suffolk to the salty ocean views of Virginia Beach. We eventually settled on the middle. A city called Chesapeake offered great schools, splendid shopping, decent access to the freeway, affordable land and was a bit off the beaten path without being too far from civilization. I picked a few school districts and wrote to a real estate agent to setup a time to review lots in the future. I also began writing to a number of builders, since I planned to take a few days off in January to meet with some builders about building our forever home. Our family was finally on the right trajectory.

W e knew Rebecca would need surgery soon, so we weren't surprised when the doctor told us in January that it was time. We also weren't ready. Taking your kid in for heart surgery is scary, even at Yale, and even with a surgeon using a Giant Microbes plush to explain the process. We also couldn't wait any longer. Rebecca was growing well, but her heart's Atrial Septal Defect (that hole connecting the upper chambers of the heart) and her malformed Tricuspid Valve made her heart struggle to give her body enough oxygenated blood. She could literally outgrow her hearts capacity if she didn't have surgery.

We slated surgery for February 8, 2017. I had already taken Rebecca to surgery once, to have a more permanent gastrointestinal tube (G-tube) installed, which made it easier to feed her. She had the nasal tube in for so long the doctors were worried about it damaging her throat, so they wanted a tube installed directly to her stomach with a small "button" that we could plug into. I had taken Rebecca to Yale and spent the night sleeping on the couch while she recovered. Her surgery was simple, but I learned firsthand that Yale, similar to most hospitals, doesn't make much in terms of accommodations for parents staying overnight. The sofa I slept on was hard, and the constant beeping of equipment made it hard to sleep. That beeping...seriously, at some point, someone needs to make medical device notifications not so horrid. After the doctors finally released Rebecca, I took her home, freed from the task of threading the G-tube down her nose.

Heart surgery was different. Rebecca would have her Atrial Septal Defect (ASD) closed. That part was about as straight forward as possible for heart surgery. The malformed tricuspid valve, well, not so much. We asked our surgeon how many kids he had seen with such a valve before. He recalled two, and talked a lot about the valve and the different methods to try and correct it. I refocused our conversation on the kids, and the surgeon told us that both kids ended up dying. Not exactly inspiring confidence. For Rebecca's surgery, the surgeon asserted he would likely leave the tricuspid valve alone, because it might adjust to the ASD closure. Rachel and I were satisfied with less surgery. It seemed much safer.

The previous month had been house-busy. I took leave and drove down to Virginia, where I spent two days interviewing builders. Having completed my requirements list, having watched every Matt Risinger YouTube video, and having read every article on concrete, door locks and a variety of other home building subjects, I had lined up times to meet with builders and interview them.

The first thing I noticed is that most small builders were terrible at returning phone calls. I had called nearly twenty builders, but only a handful, maybe seven, had returned phone calls.

Chapter 9
February 2017

During a January checkup at Yale Hospital, the doctor told us it was time to schedule surgery. Part of me was excited. Finally, Rebecca would have her heart fixed. She would finally have more energy and the right level of oxygen saturation in her blood. I had spent a lot of time with Rebecca sleeping on my chest after her therapy sessions. The poor girl was always exhausted. I wanted her to feel normal.

The other, larger part of me felt dread. Heart surgery is no joke. It boggles my mind that we can operate in someone's heart and they can live through the procedure. In preparation for surgery, I began asking people to pray for Rebecca's recovery. This was made easier because of my blogging position I had taken a few months back. While I had stayed at the hospital apartment, I had interviewed for a blogging position at a blog known as DaTechGuy. I had stumbled across him when he posted an analysis of how much bacon you would have to eat to raise your chance of colon cancer by one percent (hint: it's a lot, around a pound a day). His articles were interesting and from a Catholic perspective, so when he put out a call for new writers, I interviewed and got a position.

We scheduled surgery for Wednesday, February 8. I took the day off of work and made the now-familiar drive to Yale. After Rebecca got dressed in the prep room, the surgeon came in, described the procedure that we had already heard a thousand times over, and then we placed Rebecca in a nurse's arms and off they went. Rebecca could tell something was different, because she stared longingly at us with a puzzled face. Rachel and I walked out to go sit in the surgery recovery waiting room and tried not to cry.

Hours later, and great news: surgery was successful. Now it was a waiting game. The surgeon wanted to see progress over the next few days, so we wouldn't bring her home until Sunday or Monday. It sucked leaving the hospital again with an empty car seat, but after visiting her in the recovery room, we headed home.

During this time, I had been hunting for land to build our home. Most residential homes sit on about a quarter of an acre of land. That's enough land to squish a 2,000 square foot house on, have a backyard that kids can run around in, and a side yard that requires a fence if you want any privacy. I had lived in plenty of homes like this, and I didn't care for them one bit, for a lot of reasons.

First, I really don't relish the ability to see into my neighbor's house. For all I know, they are running a methamphetamines laboratory, or engaging in some other sort of illicit business. If I see anything, the neighbors might have Tony the local garbageman pay me a visit, and visits from Tony are always unpleasant, if you know what I mean. If it's not Tony the garbageman, then I might instead live next door to Nancy the nosy neighbor and homeowner's association president, who will kindly inform me via a letter on my door that my grass is too long, or I left the garbage can out for Tony on the wrong day, or my mulch isn't the right shade of brown. Seriously, those are real complaints I've had.

Since I'm complaining, let's talk about homeowners' associations. We live in America, but somehow the Bolshevik revolution snuck in and, not being able to form a real political party, decided to form homeowner associations. HOAs, as they are known, are horrible associations that allow petty people like Nancy your nosy neighbor to enforce all sorts of rules on your house that you purchased. Did you want to move a tree in your front yard? Better get a "permit" from the HOA for that. Are you changing the oil on your car in the driveway? You might get a ticket for a "disabled vehicle." To make matters worse, you pay fees to your HOA overlords every month! HOAs are the evil Lord Voldemort from Harry Potter that everyone can agree are seriously trying to tear apart the fabric of society.

So, no HOAs for me. Which means I have to find a lot of land on my own, since almost all new neighborhoods require that you enter into a HOA agreement. I do feel the need to specify that I don't hate people. I wasn't looking to build a house out in the boonies, away from all of humanity while I prepped for the coming zombie apocalypse. I enjoy having neighbors. I just don't enjoy being right on top of my neighbors. In Suffolk, I had lived on a half an acre of land in a neighborhood, and it was just about right, except for the dumb HOA and our nosy neighbor that sent us garbage can notices.

I began my search on Zillow, a real estate website, for a lot that was one to five acres in size and somewhat close to neighbors. I thought it would be fairly easy to find something in this range. I was wrong. It seemed there were only two sizes of land: quarter acre lots or ten-plus acre farms. I would have been okay with more acreage, but all the large lots were out in the middle of nowhere. In fact, I developed a test for lot locations called the "out of milk" test. If Google Maps declared it took longer than fifteen minutes to drive to a store that had milk, then the lot was too far out. The "store" part was flexible, so I included convenience stores like your local 7-11.

I did stumble across a set of three acre lots that looked super promising. It appeared to take a neighborhood setup and it passed my "out of milk" test. I clicked on the property, and Zillow listed the lot for thirty-thousand dollars. Whoa. That was a really great deal. I filled out my information and sent it to the real estate agent. I was really excited.

Then I remembered the rule that there were no really great deals in real estate. I did some more digging. Sure enough, those lots were involved in some sort of lawsuit with the Army Corps of Engineers. The developer had been caught illegally filling in wetlands, and the Army stopped all development. There were plenty of articles online saying that "development was coming soon," but I had no desire to become entangled in a lawsuit with the federal government.

I did receive an email reply from a real estate agent, Nadine, who confirmed the lawsuit. We discussed other property, and despite the difficulty, she developed a list of nearly a dozen lots that might work for me. I made arrangements to travel in late February to give enough time for Rebecca to recover. My house was starting to feel very real now.

Chapter 10
February 2017

Normally Fridays are fun. Not this one. Rebecca's left lung collapsed, she spiked a fever, and then the ventricle portion of her heart started beating out of sync. Yale doctors quickly stabilized her, but we were told it might mean that she would need a pacemaker installed and another surgery. That dashed all our hopes of a quick recovery. The Yale team expected at least a week of recovery in their Pediatric Intensive Care Unit, or PICU for short.

Since I would be at work, I took the whole family up to see her on Sunday after church. We had asked for a lot of prayers, and I probably had an army of people praying for Rebecca. I had a group of people I emailed about Rebecca's condition on a regular basis. We had plenty of local parishioners from our church, to include some monks from a nearby monastery that drove to Yale and prayed over her while she was still in the NICU. Every time I felt weary from driving to Yale yet again, I tried to remind myself that I had a massive support network of people that were physically and spiritually there to help Rebecca, and that network kept me going on the rough days.

Each of my kids spent time on Sunday rubbing Rebecca's head, holding her hand and talking with her while she lay on the PICU recovery bed. We brought in a giant version of the Giant Microbes Heart, which was nearly as large as her, and it provided a nice distraction to an otherwise bleak situation. After a few hours, Rebecca drifted back to sleep, and we left for home.

I returned to work on Monday. Work starts with a gym workout. February is pretty cold in Connecticut, but I always drove into work in gym clothes since the gym is across the street from my office. After a solid workout, I dashed back across the street, showered and changed, then walked into my office. I had just started to login to the computer when Rachel called and said we had to go to Yale. Now.

Rebecca's heart had gone into heart block. Normally blood flows between the atrium (top portions) and ventricle (bottom portions) because of the pressure difference in each. That pressure difference wasn't building up in Rebecca's heart, so the blood was just sitting there. If blood doesn't move, the body can't absorb oxygen from the lungs into the blood, nor can that oxygenated blood move around the body and keep it alive.

We arrived quickly at the hospital, and the doctors recommended installation of a temporary pacemaker. We authorized it and helped wheel Rebecca back for surgery. Thirty minutes later, a nurse summoned us from the waiting room to another room. As we sat there, the "Code Blue" alarm roared through the hospital, and a doctor rushed into our room, looked me straight in the eye, and coldly stated that Rebecca was in cardiac arrest. He could keep her heart on bypass or try compressions, but he needed a decision from me.

As I have mentioned before, I'm not a doctor. I don't understand the intricacies of the human body beyond a high school level. I trust other really smart people to make those decisions, especially when they are life and death decisions. The doctor's request shocked me. Luckily, time seemed to slow down so that my brain could grasp what was happening. I looked the doctor straight in the eyes and declared as confidently as I could muster "You walk into that room and you make the best damn medical decision, and I will stand by you."

Then I sat down on the floor. Rachel had essentially crumpled onto the floor in shock, and after the doctor walked out, we were alone. Listening to the Code Blue go off, knowing it is for your own child, and sitting on the cold floor of a bland colored hospital room, I cannot describe in words how absolutely lonely and lost I felt right then. I sat down and started praying, mainly because I didn't know what else to do. What was I supposed to do? Most people only see this stuff in a movie, where it's a short section, a montage of short videos, and then the plot of the movie moves forward. Not here. I sat on the chilly hospital floor with my wife while an eternity passed.

Then the Code Blue stopped. A nurse came running in to tell us that Rebecca's heart had recovered on its own. We walked out to see her alive, on a bed, being wheeled in to have pacing wires placed. Pacing wires hook up to a box outside the body that monitors the heart and delivers small impulses to keep it firing correctly.

Rebecca looked lost and scared, so we talked to her as she was wheeled in for surgery. Another hour later, this time spent on a couch with a flower pattern that was popular in 1972, and Rebecca was back in the PICU recovery room.

During that hour I had texted the nearby priest, Father John Paul Walker, about Rebecca's condition. He asked me if I wanted him to stop by to perform an emergency Confirmation. For the non-Catholics reading this, we have seven Sacraments, and Confirmation celebrates a baptized person choosing (or confirming) to enter the Church. It's normally given in eighth or ninth grade. I had never heard of an emergency Confirmation, and I didn't want to make decisions for Rebecca that I felt she had to make later in life. Father Walker, knowing I had taught Confirmation classes before, teased me about wanting to subject Rebecca later in life to a horrible Confirmation teacher. I chuckled, agreed that her critical condition probably warranted a legitimate emergency, and asked him to perform the Confirmation.

At this point it was dinner time. I was still in uniform, and both Rachel and I were starving. Rebecca was in critical but stable condition. We drove home, grabbed dinner along the way, and got back a bit before nine p.m. On a whim, we called the hospital. They told us to come immediately. I didn't even change out of my uniform before departing once again for Yale. Rachel stayed on the phone with the hospital, and there was a lot of "I understand…" and "I authorize…" conversations going on. My mind started to panic, and my heart was racing.

We sprinted into the hospital, rushed up to the PICU level, and walked in on the throng of doctors, nurses and specialists in the room. A doctor was compressing Rebecca's chest and nurses were scrambling to administer drugs. The display above Rebecca was alarming, and the heartbeat number, a green digit, read zero. I blurted out "Why is that number zero?" Right then, everything stopped. The doctor perched over Rebecca stopped the compressions, looked up at me and shook his head.

Rebecca Yvonne Haag died on February 13, 2017 at 10:15 p.m. Everything in her room was perfect. The pacing wires to her heart were firing correctly. The doctors and nurses were some of the best in the world. The second her heart had malfunctioned, a doctor had been at her side doing perfect chest compressions. I had the "A" team with the best equipment. None of that mattered, because Rebecca was not coming back.

As I stared at the hospital bed that held my daughter, still bewildered as to why her heart rate number registered as zero, the doctor and nurses slowly filtered out of the room. I heard the anesthesiologist walk out, slump into a nearby chair and sob uncontrollably. Everyone looked shell shocked. Soon there was only one nurse left, and I looked at her and sheepishly asked if I could hold Rebecca one last time. Actually, I probably just babbled some incoherent nonsense, but the nurse figured it out, bless her soul. Wiping away a small tear, she tenderly picked up Rebecca and set her in my arms. She seemed so small with all the equipment still hooked up to her. I squeezed her hand, wanting the squeeze to be returned as it had so many times before. I wanted a miracle to happen right there, for the doctor and nurses to come streaming back in because the minute I held my daughter, her heart would start back up. We'd prove everyone wrong, that the love I had for my daughter would conquer Down Syndrome and a defective heart.

It wasn't to be. I wasn't getting the happy movie ending. Rebecca wouldn't be on some successful poster outside the PICU. Her case wouldn't be encouragement to anyone. Instead, I would sit in an uncomfortable hospital chair, in my Navy uniform, disheveled from the emotional roller coaster that today had been, and I would clutch my daughter for what I knew was the last time.

Rachel and I stayed with Rebecca for an hour. We spent that time cradling her in our arms, gently stroking her head and whispering to her that we wished we could have done more. I took some pictures of her with my phone, not to share with the world, but to capture her one last time. I just, wasn't prepared to let go, wasn't prepared to walk out of that room knowing we would have an empty car seat. But eventually we both knew we had to leave. Rebecca's body, already small at seven months, was getting cold, despite my attempts to keep her warm. I knew I couldn't do anything more, that all my efforts had been for nothing, that the best hospital, insurance, medical care and effort on my part was for naught. I walked out with Rachel, utterly defeated. The drive home was hard, but by that point, I wasn't crying, because I was so drained. We didn't return home until nearly midnight.

S leep that night was rough. The next morning, I was up early, and I walked into my son's room. I climbed up into his bed and curled up next to him. He woke up, looked at me and asked, with a bit of a smile on his face, how Rebecca was doing. I told him "Neil, I'm sorry, but Rebecca didn't make it. She died last night." We then spent the next half hour crying. It was perhaps the simplest, and most difficult conversation I've ever had.

One thing I had done, somewhat incoherently, was make sure to tell others quickly about Rebecca's death. At a previous command, a co-worker had lost their first baby shortly after birth. About a week earlier, I had hosted him and his wife at our house for dinner. When I hadn't heard from him in a while, I texted him asking if the new baby had arrived yet. Getting the uncomfortable "You haven't heard" text, followed with death details, made me stop what I was doing, sit out on my porch and just hold my head. I felt so stupid, so ashamed to have happily texted him, blissfully ignorant to the obvious pain he was going through. I later learned that our command at the time was trying to preserve some privacy, but you can't hide your child's death. I had already talked with both sets of parents and a few close friends, but we had a pretty large extended network that cared about us and needed to hear the bad news. So, at nine minutes after midnight, before I curled up in my bed to try and sleep, I had posted on Facebook:

"I'm sorry everyone. Rebecca didn't make it. Please keep us in your prayers. We will reach out with more information as we go along, for now, we just need some time."

After I walked out of my son's room, I knew I needed to stay active, doing something. First it was making breakfast for everyone, not that they would eat much of it, but it was still something. While I was standing in the kitchen, I realized I had to start planning a funeral. But how to start? It's not like I had ever read about planning a funeral. That was something that old, aging people thought about, and those people had plenty of time to plan funerals in advance. I did not. As I stood there grasping for ideas, I saw the church bulletin, and a mental "Duh" flashed in my head.

Mercifully, the church secretary answered the phone. After a quick good morning, I said "Ma'am, I'm sorry to thrust this on you, but my seven-month-old daughter died last night, and I don't know how to plan a funeral. Do you have a recommendation for a funeral home?" I felt dumb for asking for a recommendation. Was my church supposed to be some sort of Yelp for funeral homes? She told me she couldn't recommend a particular funeral home, but that the funeral homes that advertised in the parish bulletin were "very good." That was enough for me, and I called and scheduled an appointment for that afternoon.

My doorbell rang shortly after, and Lezlie was at the door with a grocery bag of food. Lezlie was always professional. She always dressed smartly and composed herself well. This morning was no different, but it was obvious she had been crying earlier. She told me that the bad news had been put out at my command and my Sailors were mobilizing to help us. One Sailor called her to say, "Commander Haag always helps us and cares about our families, and I want to do something to help him." That made me proud, and a bit weak in my knees. After some coffee and small talk with Rachel and I, Lezlie left. Not unlike myself, she had to stay active doing something, and organizing support for my family was top on her list.

The next couple of days were a blur. Family and friends came into town. I signed lots of medical forms authorizing an autopsy so that Rebecca's heart problems might save someone else down the road. I organized a funeral. I attended a wake, and people packed the place. Friends came from everywhere to support us. We buried Rebecca in a donated grave site in a historic cemetery. A friend of ours organized a massive response in the Down Syndrome community. People bought meals, sent flowers, and put money in a GoFundMe account, which was important since we would have to eventually pay to move Rebecca from a grave in Connecticut to our future home.

Our future home. Forever home. Without my daughter.

It had taken me a while to accept that Rebecca's Down Syndrome might result in her permanently living in my house. Then there was the emotional drain of multiple medical appointments at Yale. Two-hour round trips sitting in traffic wore at my nerves. So too did reinserting gavage tubes in the middle of the night. The worst was still fixing that darn pump with its incessant beeps and complicated buttons. It was maddening, but I did it because I thought that in the end, I would build a house that we would all love as a family, and when Rebecca grew up, she could live comfortably with us.

Rebecca's death shattered those pleasing thoughts. Suddenly, when I thought about building a house, I felt heartbroken, angry and guilty. In the hospital with Rebecca, at times I was extremely bored and had spent that time on my phone, browsing the internet or texting friends. Mostly, I just didn't want to be there. I wanted Rebecca to be home, at my house, away from the hospital. At my home, it was easy to snuggle with her on the couch, watching the latest YouTube video about how to build your home's foundation or what type of roof to use while Rebecca dozed off on my chest. I was most comfortable at home. Yale, for all its accolades, was just an uncomfortable place to be. Since I always thought we would go home eventually, I just wished the doctors would hurry up, do their thing and let us go. Suddenly, that time was gone, and I ached over every minute I had spent on the phone instead of stroking Rebecca's head or holding her hand.

I could not get that time back. Worse, as the funeral ended and family members began to head home, I had to make a decision: do I continue with house plans? It was now February 22, the day after Rebecca's funeral, and I had planned to drive down the next day and stay with my friend Chris to begin looking at property in the area. I had planned to meet a real estate agent, Nadine, for the first time. I could cancel all these plans, and who would judge me for it?

But I sat down with Rachel first, and we talked. We talked about our future. We came to grips with the fact that our future did not include having Rebecca with us, and that the best we could do was find a way to have her buried near us. Rachel did not want me to have to work extra hard on our future home. We had already done so much, and to not get a break seemed unfair. But I remembered that life isn't fair. Most people don't live a life without challenges, and if you've ever had goals in life, you probably had to work hard to achieve them. When I asked Rachel about her goal of finally settling down in our own home, I could see the fire in her eyes. The longest I had lived in one place was thirty-two months, and on average we moved to a new state every twenty months. The wear and tear moving took on our stuff and our sanity was beginning to show. Rachel still wanted to move forward with our house plans, so I continued packing the car for Virginia.

Chapter 12
February 2017

On a chilly, dark February morning at 3:30 a.m., I pulled out of my driveway. It was just above freezing, and my car kindly reminded me, through another annoying beep, to be careful when driving on frozen roads. I pulled up to our friendly Gales Ferry Dunkin' Donuts, grabbed a large hot latte, and jumped on I-95 South. There was almost nobody on the road, and before long I was crossing the George Washington Bridge, the last major hurdle before I was on open freeway. Sleeping in the passenger seat next to me was my brother-in-law Mark. Mark had ridden the train to New London to attend Rebecca's funeral, but had been too unwell to travel back alone. I offered to drive him to Richmond, Virginia where he lived, since it was along the way back.

Mark and I have extremely different personalities. When I took the Myers-Briggs test, I came out in the middle of introvert and extrovert. That means I was strengthened from both group interactions and from being alone. It makes me pretty versatile and adaptable. Mark, on the other hand, is a true introvert. He can eat dinner with you and barely utter three sentences in an hour and be perfectly content. It's not that he doesn't enjoy the company. He is just truly content to say few words. On our car ride down over a five-hour period, between sleeping and listening to music, I don't think Mark talked for more than twenty minutes.

Luckily, our early departure made it easy to beat traffic. I pulled off the freeway into Richmond, dropped Mark off at his car, and jumped back on the freeway. Driving on I-64 takes you onto a fairly quiet peninsula before you arrive in the Hampton Roads area. There isn't much except trees, water and the cement freeway between the outskirts of Richmond and the beginnings of Williamsburg. Once I was steady on the freeway, I set cruise control, merged into the center lane, and cried. Hard. Tears just streamed out. I had nothing else to think about but Rebecca's funeral. I cried over shutting her casket for the last time. I cried about all the time I had wasted in the hospital. I cried about all the effort I had put in to keeping her alive, only to have her snatched away. I cried about how helpless I felt, that somehow the best medical team in the world couldn't keep my baby girl alive. I thought about how unfair life was to me, that I had fought for Rebecca from her conception, when the hospital in Hawaii was quick to say she should be aborted because she wasn't growing at their expected rate, or when the Yale doctor offered to terminate her because of her heart malfunction. All that fighting, all that effort, and here I was, in an empty, quiet car on a freeway in Virginia, with nothing to show for it.

That part of the car ride was long and painful. It was also probably the best thing for me. I needed time to myself, because after the crying came rage. I was angry at everything. Angry at the surgeons, with their fancy degrees and smarts, that couldn't fix Rebecca's broken heart. Furious at all my efforts, all the stress my wife endured, all of it being for nothing. I cursed an awful lot in the car. Four letter words spit out from my mouth like bullets from a gun. Thankfully, only the trees heard my swearing, and I kept the cruise control set to prevent speeding. The long car ride grew shorter, my rage slowly abated, the tears slowly dried up, and soon I was crossing the Monitor-Merrimac Bridge Tunnel heading towards Suffolk.

My friend Chris lives out in farm country in Suffolk. I had first met Chris in 2008 while working at the Navy's Second Fleet command in Norfolk. Chris would occasionally come to brief Rear Admiral Scott Sanders, who I worked for directly, and on occasion I stopped by his desk to pick up updated briefing materials from him. I noticed that he had pictures of North Korea on his desk, and he told me about how he was stationed on the North Korea border at a previous assignment. Later that year, my wife and I watched a National Geographic Explorer film called "*Inside North Korea.*" In the documentary, there is a part where a U.S. military officer tries catch the attention of the North Korean guards so that they could accept the remains of a North Korean soldier recently exhumed in South Korea that had died during the Korean War. When the North Koreans refuse to answer their shared phone line, a Navy officer grabs a megaphone and begins loudly demanding for an answer from the North Korean guards.

That officer had a really, really distinctive voice. So distinctive that I paid attention and noticed his

Navy camouflage uniform. I stopped the video and zoomed in. The last name matched. At work, I stopped by Chris' desk and asked him, and he sheepishly acknowledged his five minutes of fame. So, I was essentially shacking up at a movie star's house, or at least that's how I viewed the situation.

I pulled up to Chris' house deep in the Suffolk farmland. Chris was a newlywed and an aspiring hops farmer that, after retiring from the Navy, had purchased seven acres of land and was working on putting up poles to start his organic hops farm. He was also Rebecca's godfather, and was one of the first people I had called after she died. I had texted him and he met me at the door. I got about three words into greeting him when he asked how I was doing. I then spent the next several minutes in a bear hug while I sobbed tears on his shoulder.

We sat, drank and talked. Chris appreciates hand crafted beer as much as I do, and he has dogs that beg for scratches behind their ears, and what I needed right then was a tasty drink and a positive way to relieve my stress. Beer was consumed, dog ears were scratched, and eventually the day ended with less tears and more positive feelings about the future.

The next morning, I left early to meet Nadine. I had talked with her briefly over the phone, and we agreed to meet in Chesapeake at our first site. I had resolved to not talk about Rebecca with her, only because I felt that was an awful lot to dump on someone at our first meeting. As I stepped out of the car, I saw Nadine parked in front. She was an older lady, medium height, and had a bright face and warm smile. We shook hands and walked onto the first property.

It was a wooded three-and-a-half acres off of a connector road between two main roads. It had plenty of residential development around it, including a large residential neighborhood being built next door by a well-known builder. The woods were decently thick, but I could walk along the edge to gauge the lot depth and makeup. Instantly, I really, really liked it. It was near people without being on top of them. It was near shopping without being so close. It was near the freeway without the freeway noise. It passed the "out of milk" test.

I told myself to not fall in love with the first place I saw. We both returned to our cars, punched in the GPS coordinates and headed to the next place, a four-and-a-half-acre lot near Hickory Elementary School. The lot bordered a freeway, but the trees were thick enough you couldn't hear it. You also didn't hear much else because it was pretty far out in farm country. I noticed it was almost ten minutes from any stores, the nearest being a 7-11. Now, nothing against 7-11, but if you need extensive groceries, 7-11 is likely not your first shopping venue choice. So back on the road we went.

Onto the next place, which was a lot inside a Kibor Homes development. The lots were OK, but they were devoid of trees and extremely exposed. It's looked as if someone took an enormous farm, cleared everything around it, and air dropped a neighborhood on top. It looked like that, because that's exactly what had happened. Most of the new developments we drove by were former farms carved up by a developer.

That sort of lot didn't have the privacy I wanted. One neighborhood had a beautiful blue home with a detached two-car garage that had an apartment over the garage. I stopped to stare because the home setup was perfect. It looked, at least on the outside, like everything I wanted in a home. It was also about ten feet from another house. It reminded me of an old black and white photo in a history text book that showed two New Yorkers shaking hands from their windows. It just didn't seem right to place a large, beautiful house on such a small lot of land.

We kept viewing lots. All in all, that day Nadine showed me almost twenty lots. Most didn't pass the "out of milk" test, and it became obvious that one to five acres was a difficult lot size to find. By the time we finished, we were far away from the first place, near a pig farm. Yup, a smelly pig farm. Not my idea of forever home. That lot was near two other custom homes though, and the owner of one house came outside to see what we were doing. When I explained, she gleefully shared her builders contact information with me. Her house was beautiful, sporting a nice metal roof and sitting on an encapsulated crawl space. Overjoyed to have more builder options, I wrote down the builder's information before leaving the stunning view of a bacon-making facility. On my way back to Chris' house, I was excited to finally have at least a few land options and a potential new builder.

Chapter 13

Custom builders are terrible at returning phone calls. Did I mention that before? If I did, I think it needs mentioning again. While I was fairly certain that Manicured Homes was going to work for me, I wanted options. I called a ton of other builders. Nadine even recommended a couple builders. My other friends recommended builders. I found builders on the internet. I called, and called, and called. Some people called back. Some builders called back once, then disappeared. Some disappeared, only to call again after going dark for two months. I felt confused every time the phone rang. Which builder are you? What had we talked about? I ended up keeping a notebook of every builder I had called just to help me remember who was who in my building zoo.

Every time another builder blew off my phone call, I realized the appeal of using a larger company like Manicured Homes. It is totally frustrating to be excited about building a new home, only to have a small builder appear to blow off your hopes and dreams. Customer service, and a person to just answer the darn phone, did not appear on the list of custom builder requirements. I would call a business, say, Eagle Home Building, and they would make all sorts of promises. "We can totally beat that price," Eagle Home Building would tell me on the phone. That would make me excited! Then, I wouldn't hear from them. I'd call back, and no one would answer. That cycle would repeat with many other builders. Finally, after about a month of trying to line up other builder options, I eventually decided that Manicured Homes was going to be my builder.

I also trusted my gut instinct and picked the first forested lot Nadine had shown me. After driving back to Connecticut, I compared all the lots that passed the "out of milk" test, looking at schools, distance to work, proximity to neighbors and a few other things that Rachel and I cared about. The forested lot won out on all points. It also just felt right. It's hard to explain, but walking around it and driving around the area, I had a weird, satisfied feeling about the lot. Since the hard numbers and feelings both matched, I felt really good about my choice.

Now that I had a lot and a home builder, it was time for paperwork. If you've bought a home before you probably remember the mountain of paperwork you had to sign and the process that this paperwork followed. Constructing a new home also involves paperwork, but the process is significantly different. When you buy an already-built home, you first find the house you want and put in an offer. This starts a negotiation on price with the owner, and after some back and forth, you settle on a price and sign a contract. Then some legal people go through a checklist and prepare documents. Someone will do a title search to make sure the right person owns the home. Someone else checks for liens against the property, in case the owner didn't pay someone for work completed.

A home inspector comes out and makes sure the house is up to code. An appraiser comes out and assesses the value of the house, so that the bank making the loan doesn't lend out more money than the home is worth.

Once all the individuals have come back, you arrive for a final signing day. You sit down with a notary and go through a stack of documents. They are all printed on 8.5 by 14-inch paper, because lawyers need that extra three inches to say what would normally fit on a regular sheet of paper. The notary and you go through the stack page by page, initialing and signing, making sure to sign your name exactly as it appears under the line. As you approach the end, your hand is cramping and your vision is blurring, when suddenly the notary says "Congratulations, you're a home owner!" Balloons and confetti drop from the ceiling, and suddenly you and your family start dancing the Harlem Shake. That last part is made up, I'm betting that hasn't happened to you. You're just excited to be done with the pain of paperwork, and maybe you walked out and had a nice dinner when it was finally over.

Building a home from scratch is a bit different. Once you've found a builder and a lot, you have to make an offer on the lot. During that time, you're working to arrange financing for the lot and the soon-to-be-built home. Once the owner of the lot accepts your offer, you get a stream of people that appear as if summoned by magic to create sheets of paper you didn't realize were required to build a home. One of those people is a surveyor, who lays out where the home will sit on the property. An assessor will look at the survey, and the lot, and the building plans and make an educated guess as to the final worth of the home. This assessment goes to the bank, and the bank issues a Construction to Permit loan. This CP loan, as it is called, is way different than a normal loan. It starts life as a twelve-month interest-only loan on the property. You make interest-only payments each month based on the principal of the loan. As the builder builds a section of the house, say the foundation, he or she will make a draw on the loan, which means they ask the bank to pay them for the work completed. You as the owner sign the draw, the builder gets paid, and the principal grows. Once the builder finishes, they make a final draw and the loan converts into a standard thirty-year fixed mortgage.

If you're doing the math in your head and think, wow, that sounds expensive, you're right! Grab a cookie from the smart reader cookie jar, you earned it! This process is not for the faint of heart, and not for people that don't have some money sitting around. Previously, I had been stationed in Hawaii. Hawaii is an extremely expensive place to live. Housing, electricity, restaurants, and everyday living is costly, and it's so expensive the government gives you extra money, called a Cost of Living Adjustment, or COLA, to compensate for these expenses. Unlike many people that simply blow through this money, I looked at how to save it. My family lived in base housing, which was free. The housing unit had metered electricity, so you had a base number of kilowatt hours you could use without getting charged. I looked up the sunrise and sunset times and adjusted the solar water heater and air conditioning settings to better match that solar cycle. It was effective enough that my house of three kids and a wife used the same electricity as the next-door neighbor with no kids, and we still used air conditioning during the day.

I combined that with a lot of smart shopping. My wife shopped almost exclusively at the commissary, which was twenty to fifty percent cheaper than shopping out in town. We also soon learned where all the family-friendly restaurants were in the nearby area. My kids aren't picky eaters, and soon we had scouted out our favorite Ramen and Sushi places in Hawaii-Kai, the local malls, on the nearby Air Force base, and up on the Northern Shore. We enjoyed Hawaii without it killing our pocket books, and all that extra COLA got stashed away for a rainy day.

I called up Manicured Homes and scheduled a time to sign paperwork. Since I had to do this in person, I went back on leave, drove the eight hours to Suffolk and stayed at Chris' house again. I walked into Manicured Homes' office the next day and the paperwork began. Steve walked me through the initial paperwork. He was working with Nadine directly to bid on the lot. I signed forms that declared I would work with Manicured Homes to build a house on that lot or a nearby lot (in case the deal fell through) and paid 250 dollars as an application fee. It was surprisingly simple, way less complicated than I expected.

I walked out after signing and called Nadine. She was pleased for me, but then she asked "So who is designing your house?" My brain locked up. I had been so focused on getting a builder and a lot that I hadn't really finalized my house designer. "Not to worry," she told me, "I think I have you covered."

Chapter 14
April 2017

It's not like I hadn't put any thought towards designing my house. I had been thinking about it. I had put together requirements for the house: five bedrooms, a guest suite downstairs, L-shaped open concept, peninsula-style wood fireplace, an office for me, a craftroom for Rachel, and a mudroom for our sanity. All of this thinking hadn't translated into getting someone to actually put pen to paper and design the place. Thankfully, Nadine hooked me up with Otto.

I emailed Otto and we agreed to meet in April. I talked with him on the phone and I admitted that while I had requirements, I had no idea how to start laying out a house. When I would watch fancy home designer shows, the design portion just magically happened. Here is the typical scene: the host starts talking, saying something fancy like "We're going to have the foyer flow into the dining room...", then the TV screen would shift to a cartoon pencil, drawing the foyer's gentle flow into the dining area on a sheet of graph paper, complete with pencil drawing "scritch scratch" sounds. As the host continues describing the first-floor layout, the cartoon pencil dutifully draws out the walls, bathrooms and flooring at blazing speed, occasionally coloring in the gaps for good effect. When the second floor comes up, the same pencil demonstrates the artistic competence of Michelangelo by drawing the three-dimensional house, bedrooms, and a walk out porch for good measure.

I suspected that Otto didn't have a magic pencil, although it would be totally awesome if he did. Instead, I asked him how to start laying out a house. On the phone, I explained that I had what I wanted for requirements, but no idea how to put it all together. "Too easy," he told me. "Start with a square, draw in rooms, then shift walls from there."

I stood in my living room dumbfounded, my mouth agape. That sounded totally easy, and this whole time I had been imagining something super complicated. So, I followed Otto's directions exactly. I drew a gigantic square on a sheet of paper and labeled it "downstairs." I then carved out rooms: a garage, mudroom, kitchen, craft room, guest suite, office, living room, and porch. Next came the upstairs square and the bedrooms, bathrooms and laundry room. I sat down with Rachel, who promptly tore up my drawings and started fresh. Just kidding, she didn't actually do that, although she moved the rooms around slightly. Having it on paper in a simple form was just pure genius.

The slightly harder part came with measurements. I started with the two-car garage, since it's easy to determine how much space you need for vehicles. After that, it was more difficult. How much space do you need in a kitchen, in terms of square feet? I spent a lot of time having Rachel stand and put her arms out, then measuring with a tape measure to comprehend what size of space she needed. This constant back and forth resembled a fashion model show, where you see the fashion model effortlessly move in the scene while the camera guy strains to take pictures of her at all the right angles. Here I was, the poor camera guy, trying to capture how much space my wife's movements would require in terms of square footage in her new kitchen. It was a strange tape measure kabuki dance, but it got the job done.

After room sizes were mostly determined, I changed the layout of two upstairs bathrooms. I had three kids, and although Rebecca had died, I was hopeful that we would have another child at some point. That many kids equals a lot of time spent in the bathrooms. We had friends with teenagers and they always complained about the long bathroom lines in the morning. Since I too would have teenagers someday, I designed our bathrooms with two doors, so that the toilet and bath was separated from the sink. This allows someone to either be taking a bath or using the toilet while another person can brush their teeth, or comb hair, or put on makeup, or do whatever else at the sink. My hope was this would make that morning rush for school a little less daunting.

I took my square drawings, scanned them in and emailed Otto, who agreed to meet the next time I was in Norfolk. I took leave and drove down in April, and we met at a bookstore in Virginia Beach. Otto was a thin athletic man with a scruffy beard, dark glasses and easy-going manner. We effortlessly walked through the project. I showed him my drawing as well as a sketch of the lot, and he wasn't worried one bit about getting the project done. He told me it would be done by early May.

I hadn't just driven down to visit Otto. Nadine had put together all the paperwork and said it was time to put an offer on the lot. I saw the list price, but it was a bit high, so I had Nadine put in a bid about forty-thousand dollars lower than asking price. The seller was apparently insulted, and after a little bit of prying we figured out why. Since the property sat next to a large suburban development, there had been many people giving low-ball offers to try and snatch it up with the intent of turning it around and selling it to the developer. A developer can fit three to four homes per acre on a lot, and a little over three acres would yield a large profit.

The owner had another logical reason to ask for a better price. His lot was one of the few to be listed with access to both city water and city sewer. Most of the lots that weren't in a residential neighborhood required septic tanks, and many required a well for water. Because the Hampton Roads area has a high-water table, you have to use a special type of septic system, which costs approximately thirty to forty-thousand dollars. Wells had mineral and rust issues that tended to clog the inside of faucets. A septic system and well would cut into my budget pretty significantly.

In contrast, the city water system was more than satisfactory. When I had previously lived there, I brewed beer with water right out of the tap. Beer is fairly sensitive to water quality. If there are too many minerals, chloramine or dissolved solids in the water, you'll taste it in your beer. One time in San Diego, I had brewed five gallons of my Firecracker Ale, which is a red ale in which I dissolve two pounds of Red Hot candies to give it a spicy, cinnamon flavor. It's the perfect beer for watching Fourth of July fireworks, sitting in your lawn chair sipping a cold beer that has a pleasant aroma and taste of cinnamon. California had other plans that year. Not only was it too dry for fireworks, but the years of poor water management practices had lowered aquifer levels. This caused a decline in drinking water quality and raised the iron content in the water. When I drank my first beer, the iron wasn't noticeable until the end, then it hit you like a freight train. It felt as if I was chewing on an iron bar, and if that image makes you cringe, it should. I had to dump the rest of the fifty beer bottles into our flower beds. Thankfully, the flowers didn't have to drive anywhere that day.

I looked up property details on the city's website. The property owner had owned this land forever, and likely had no reason to sell it quickly. Since nothing was forcing him to sell, he was going to stick to the price he wanted. He knew the city water and sewer raised the value of the property more than the other large farms that developers were carving into giant neighborhoods. But at least my low offer had elicited a counteroffer, and after some back and forth, we agreed on a price and signed a contract.

At this point, I had a builder, a lot with an accepted offer, and a home designer cranking out my home design. I sent a draft of the design to Manicured Homes, then sat back and smiled. I was well on my way to custom home ownership, and nothing could derail me on my quest.

Chapter 15
June 2017

Otto was late. His confidence that my house was a "pretty straight forward design" took longer because he was busy with his day job. I got my first draft on May 4, and while the downstairs was pretty close, the upstairs had no bedrooms. Rachel and I sent back feedback, and on May 10 we received a second draft that had both floors.

When you look at an actual set of plans, it sparks a lot of questions. My first question concerned windows. Each window had a label, like 2020 or 3030. I didn't understand what these labels meant, but YouTube had a convenient explanation. The first two numbers are the width in feet, the second two the height in feet. So, a 3030 window is three feet wide by three feet long, and a 3036 window is three feet wide by three feet and six inches tall. Imagining how a three-foot window compares to a three-foot six-inch window is not easy, so I did what any logical person would do. I printed the plans, took it to Home Depot and stood in the window aisle looking at windows of different sizes. I practiced opening and shutting each window, and envisioned it sitting in the wall, which is significantly easier to visualize when the window is sitting on the floor in front of you. I also figured if I could find the window at Home Depot, it would be easy to replace later in life if it was ever damaged.

I also had to verify all the little details, and trust me, there are a lot of details. Which way do you want the doors to swing? Which model of fireplace do you want, and are the dimensions correct? Is the tub you have the right size? What about the water heater? How high do you want the sinks in each bathroom? Do you want shutters for your windows? The list went on and on. Rachel and I poured through every set of plans, and we sent them to Rachel's mom, who had been an architect early in life. Her experience taught us to ask even more in-depth questions. For example, could we route all the pipes on internal walls? That helps prevent them from freezing.

We sent a large list of changes back on May 11, and Otto continued planning. By this point, the plans had the correct number of rooms, square footage and major details, so I felt comfortable sending them to Manicured Homes. I sent draft plans and asked Steve to verify that the house would fit inside our budget. About a week later I received a phone call saying that so long as we didn't significantly change the plans, we would be inside our budget.

The planning changes continued though. Each week I would email Otto, and each week I was promised we would be finished quickly, and each week it would not be complete. Without a final set of plans, Manicured Homes couldn't produce a final estimate. Without that, we couldn't close a construction to permit loan. Without that, the land owner had no guarantee of any sort of money. Thus, in late May, Nadine notified me that the landowner's real estate agent was asking why the process was taking so long. That's when I started to sweat a bit. I had no control over Otto's effort, and I also had no backup. Starting with someone else would be expensive and probably take longer.

Updated plans came on May 17 and May 24. The May 24 plans were pretty much final, so I asked Otto to finalize plans. He wanted to go over them in person, so I scheduled leave and prepared to drive down. I was hoping that meeting in person would expedite the process. What was supposed to take two weeks was now over a month. I drove down on June 4 and met with Otto. We reviewed the plans, finalized details and I asked him to please, please be fast finalizing plans.

I drove from our meeting over to Manicured Homes with a printed set of nearly final plans. I signed a ton of mortgage paperwork, with some spots empty to put in finalized house plans. I figured it would make that process easier if all I had to do was amend paperwork, rather than draft it from scratch. As I was preparing to leave Norfolk, Otto sent me a final set of plans on June 8. I ecstatically sent them to Manicured Homes, called Nadine to give her the heads up, and headed back to Groton.

Later that month a representative from Union Mortgage called me. Vance sounded like an experienced mortgage loan officer: smooth, composed and confident. He discussed the paperwork with me, the construction to permit (CP) loan process, and the Veteran's Affairs (VA) process as well. In terms of layers of complication, the CP loan added complications, and the VA another layer, and all these layers built a nice cake, except that the baker added two layers of Brussel sprouts to the cake as a cruel and inhumane way of enforcing their vegetable-eating habits on you, when all you wanted was a tasty slice of yummy cake. Anyway, that's how the construction loan process feels, but I managed to stomach it and move forward.

Everything was going great until I got a phone call from Manicured Homes on June 20. I picked up my cell phone in what I hoped was a fun phone call, only to have Steve give me bad news. My budget was sixty-thousand dollars short. "But if we left out cabinets, or cut out two or three rooms, we might get there." I was stunned. Leaving out kitchen cabinets? Cutting out rooms? That wasn't my dream house. Before hanging up, Steve sent me some of Manicured Homes currently offered house plans to see if I could make one work.

My shock turned to anger about an hour after I hung up the phone. I realized that Manicured Homes had never been serious about building a custom home. They had their designs that they built, and they would force me to use one, or cut my dream home down so much I wouldn't recognize it. I walked outside and balled my fists. That jerk! He screwed me. I picked up a large stick and slammed it into the trunk of a nearby tree. It snapped, sending a piece twirling off into the nearby woods. I picked up quite a few sticks and beat on that tree until I had burned off enough anger. In case you're wondering, the tree didn't care, and no bark was harmed during my little tirade.

Steve's betrayal taught me a really valuable lesson. Builders have a way of doing business, and if what you want fits in their existing model, you're good. When it doesn't, they will lie to you all the way to the bank to steal your money. Don't want to build a customer's encapsulated crawl space? Just say "nobody does that in Hampton Roads." Don't want to deal with a custom design? Simply lead the customer on, like a bull with a nose ring, until the customer is at the point of no return. In all my research, nobody talked about that finer point of the construction industry.

I was so screwed. I had a landowner angry that he hadn't been paid yet, a mortgage that needed a plan, and a builder that was patiently waiting for me to cave to his demands. I sat on my couch blankly staring at the wall, balling my fists in anger, because I had no idea what to do next.

Chapter 16

I started calling builders. Lots of other builders. On the 22nd of June I called and emailed Mr. Deon of America Builders and Mr. Manius at LuMa Construction. Then, I waited.

Waiting for a call back is agonizing. I essentially had till the end of the month, which was only 8 days away, to send a builder contract to Union Mortgage. I called Vance at Union Mortgage to ask about my options, and he didn't seem to care about Manicured Homes all that much. "I don't really care who you work with, so long as you have a quote from a reputable builder, I'll work to get you the loan," he told me on the phone. It made sense. Vance would make money if a loan closed, and he'd rather make money than not make money.

Mr. Deon called me back first. He was incredibly interested in making a deal. I had seen a home he built, the one that overlooked the pig processing plant, and had talked with the owner during my initial property search. The owner was ecstatic about her home, so that was a really good sign. I sent him the drawings and asked for a quote ASAP. I hung up the phone feeling somewhat positive.

Then Mr. Manius called. He listened to my plight with intrigue. I sent him plans and my budget, and he stated we could get to yes. I liked that answer. When I mentioned the encapsulated crawl space, he said "That is a really good idea, and yes, we've done those before."

That was the moment for me. It probably sounds totally dumb, like a poorly written line in a cheap romantic novel where the main female character falls madly in love with the dark, mysterious, and totally buff male character. Not that I would have ever read cheap romantic novels, I merely heard of such things from my female friends, and would otherwise have no knowledge whatsoever of such things. For the sake of this story, I would have been that poorly written female character, and Manius was my savior. My dream house was on the line. If I didn't have a contract, it was never going to happen. I needed a hero builder ASAP.

We chatted a lot on the phone, and I looked up both builders. Both were registered with the local Better Business Bureau, which I really liked. I had used the "triple-B" in the past to keep businesses honest. When a moving company broke my washer during my move to Hawaii and refused to compensate me, I complained to the military moving liaison. What I didn't realize was that she was a local Hawaiian and apparently hated military members, so she took the company's side. It seemed like an odd thing to do at the time, since her job title would imply caring about the military members and trying to win fair compensation for them. Luckily, I also complained to the BBB, and my complaint to the BBB drove down their online rating and forced a compromise. The fact that I had to essentially shame them online was annoying, but worth it to not take a five hundred dollar hit to my pocketbook.

I also found LuMa Construction on a local Hampton Roads Builder's Association, which gave me more hope that LuMa was in fact a legitimate company. It sounds dumb, but there are a ton of small building companies and trying to find out which one is legitimate is remarkably difficult. Once you look past the Ryan Homes and Ashford Builders of the world, you won't recognize the small company names, since most of these companies build only a dozen homes a year.

Deon never called me back. Manius did, and emailed me a quote that was inside my budget and had the details that I wanted in a house. I promptly emailed it to Vance and then called him, and he started processing right away. I was nervous. It was coming down to the wire. Vance called me back on June 29 and said that the loan processed successfully. Success at last! I called Nadine and gave her the uplifting news. Nadine then called the landowner and got an extension. Essentially, the owner was willing to wait another month since we had shown legitimate movement on the loan. I had narrowly escaped having to start all over again. The extension became official on July 1.

I sat down on the same couch I had been so frustrated on only a few days prior and slowly sipped a beer. I had beaten the clock! Yes, I was going to have to deal with a mortgage company and sign a lot of papers, but I was OK with that. As a Naval Officer, I had moved almost every two years, so I had purchased and sold a few homes in that time. I also had a variety of credit cards, vehicle loans and the occasional loan for a furniture purchase. I had plenty of credit history, which made it easy for loan companies to research my financial profile.

Even better, I had always taken steps to live within my means. When my wife and I lived in San Diego, both of us were working and we had no kids and plenty of extra money. If we wanted to eat out, we did. If we wanted to see a movie, or go shopping, we did that too. We always had enough money to do whatever we wanted. Flash forward to when we first moved to Suffolk (which is in the Hampton Roads area) and things were quite different. Rachel had shifted to become a full-time mom for our daughter. We had purchased a dog, who promptly ate four of my uniform socks and required surgery. This taught me a valuable lesson: veterinarians are in fact doctors and do in fact charge like doctors. To top it off, that was when I switched careers from submarines to cryptology and lost my very large submarine bonus.

Suddenly, the credit card wasn't paid off each month, and the balance was growing. I simply didn't have enough money to pay everything. It was a bit embarrassing that somehow, with a college degree and a job as a Naval Officer, I couldn't make ends meet. I was failing as the provider for my family. My pride took a hefty hit. But, after a bit of soul searching, my wife and I built a plan to restore our financial health. We cut a lot out of our life. Cable TV was out, and antenna TV was back in style. Eating out at will was gone, and home cooked meals made a comeback. The credit card balance monster was slowly bled to death and we regained control of our lives.

I maintained pretty good financial control from then on, and with that, I had a pretty excellent credit score. Getting people to lend me money wasn't a problem, so I could rest easy while the mortgage people worked through their various forms. I sipped my beer into the night, satisfied that I had survived the craziness.

Sure enough, July was the form of months...I mean, the month of forms. As expected, I had many forms to fill out related to the mortgage. Because my mortgage was backed by the Veteran's Administration, it required even more forms. Union Mortgage assigned Tatiana as my production coordinator and Aurelia as the mortgage processor. After a pleasant introduction email, Tatiana told me she would be taking all forms through Union Mortgage's website, which made it easy to upload forms in a safe, encrypted manner.

Tatiana's first form list was eye watering. I had to read and digitally sign a loan estimate, settlement service provider list, acknowledgement of intent to proceed, borrower's certification and authorization, equal credit opportunity act notice, fair credit reporting act, VA notice to applicants, hazard insurance authorization, home counseling agency information, a VA addendum to the uniform residential loan application, the uniform residential loan application (almost forgot that one!), an FBI warning on mortgage fraud, IRS request for tax return, net tangible benefit disclosure, social security administration authorization, US PATRIOT act information disclosure, credit score disclosure, certification of VA status, and a VA debt questionnaire.

I might have forgot one or twenty, please don't hold it against me.

I dutifully read each and every form. Yup, every one of them. The most important form was the uniform residential loan application, called the URLA. It sounds similar to "Ursula," the sea witch from "The Little Mermaid," and probably for good reason. I bet Ursula, when she wasn't practicing black magic on the ocean floor, was a mortgage loan officer. I could see her putting mortgages in front of her clients, who didn't read the fine print in the contract and signed away their future earnings for the hope of a new home built on the shaky foundation of the sea bottom. Maybe all the "poor unfortunate souls" were really underwater homeowners bilked out of their homes, broken and destitute by Ursula the Home Mortgage Witch.

Wait, where was I? Oh yeah, the URLA. It has a ton of numbers on it, ranging from the estimated home cost, closing costs, and survey cost to the final loan estimate and interest rate. I was a bit puzzled that it listed two interest rates, so I called Tatiana to ask for an explanation. She explained that the Construction to Permit loan had an interest rate for the build portion, then the final interest rate for the final loan. "Gotcha," I replied, "that makes sense to me." I kept going through the forms and unfortunately, I found some errors in the VA section, mainly distinguishing that I was still on active duty and a veteran. Tatiana made changes and resent the digital forms.

Most of the forms after the URLA were short, one- or two-page forms. They seemed to be a hodge-podge of paperwork required by a multitude of government organizations, none of which talked to each other. Take the FBI disclosure, which tells you not to engage in mortgage fraud, and that you are expected to pay back your mortgage. I guess I'm not surprised that the FBI might not look kindly on mortgage fraud, but someone, somewhere must have been surprised and thought "Gee, I should make everyone fill out a disclosure form on mortgage fraud." I cannot claw back the eight and a half minutes I spent reading that form back in my life, so whoever that person is, I hope you toss and turn in your sleep and step on a LEGO brick.

But it's not enough for the FBI to tell me to not engage in fraud. The VA has its own fraud form which says that I'm expected to make payments and pay off my loan. They kindly remind you that because the government backs the loan, they will try to recoup any loss, and if you can't make payments for some reason, you should call them first. As I read through these forms, I sarcastically thought "Are people seriously so stupid that they think they could take out a loan for hundreds of thousands of dollars, then walk away and stop paying without any repercussions?" Then I remembered that microwaves had warnings on them declaring "Not for drying cats," and the Tide laundry detergent pods had a warning stating "Do not eat this laundry soap."

I signed mountains of digital forms, killing megabytes of digital trees in my quest to build a home. Most of the forms returned to Union Mortgage without issue. But then Aurelia, the mortgage processor, emailed me back and asked if I was OK using a particular settlement agent. What made it weird is that Nadine, my real estate agent, had already sent them a particular settlement agent, who conveniently had done a survey of the property and was knowledgeable about it. For some reason, that didn't register at Union Mortgage, but I also didn't care who was the settlement agent. Settlement agents are the organizations that put together the massive stack of papers, ensuring everything is in order to meet city requirements.

If you're confused, don't feel bad, and a review of all the characters currently in my story is probably timely right now. I've got Nadine, my real estate agent, who found the property and works with the property owner to let me purchase the land. I've got a builder, Manius, from LuMa Construction, who will build the physical house. I then have Vance, Tatiana and Aurelia from Union Mortgage, who will finance the home building and land buying with a loan. And lastly, I now have Cassia, from Homes Etc., who will put together all forms and supervise the transfer of assets in this process.

My merry band being assembled, now I could now sit back, relax, and enjoy the home building process. Just kidding, this would be a short book if that was true! Do you remember when I briefly mentioned that Vance would work with any reputable builder? Well, "reputable builder" is defined as someone that filled out forms (always more forms!) and was registered as a builder in their system. So, while the mortgage was processing, Vance called me to ask about this form. "Ryan, I need you to get your builder to fill out the builder application," implying that he had already sent the form a while back and Manius was being a slacker. OK, no big deal. I texted Manius and asked him nicely to remember to fill out the Union Mortgage builder application.

Manius promptly called me back and stated he didn't have any forms. Weird. Now I felt a bit trapped in the middle. I had to work with everyone, and I certainly didn't need infighting in my merry band of home builders. I decided to use an old trick from my Navy staff experience. I emailed Vance and Manius on the same email and asked Vance to "reply all" with the forms. What it did was ensure that everyone was communicating about the same thing. Vance sent the forms, so now I had copies of the forms and I knew that Manius had received them. Manius finished the forms promptly, and all problems were resolved. Even better, Vance called me the next day (July 20) to inform me I was conditionally approved for the mortgage.

But we were not done with forms. Aurelia emailed me to request a few more documents, namely my military orders to the Hampton Roads area and the flood determination for the house. The property had two flood zones. The back of the property was in flood zone AE, which meant that each year there was a 1 percent chance of flooding. Because math in public is hard, I'll just tell you that this translates to a twenty-six percent chance of flooding over the life of a thirty-year mortgage. That's high enough to merit purchasing flood insurance and can raise the cost of your home. However, the front part of the property is in zone X500, which means that it annually has a flood rate of less than 0.2%, which translates to a flooding event once every five hundred years. Obviously, these odds are better, and doesn't require flood insurance, and the mortgage company needed a map showing where the house would be located. I figured this would be taken care of by the builder.

I was wrong. Aurelia emailed me asking for something showing where the house would be. In a flash of inspiration, I printed a copy of the flood zone map, drew a box in the shape of my house, labeled it with an arrow, and sent it back. It looked like something one of my kids would draw at school, but I thought why not, maybe it'll work.

My 2nd grade level house location sketch didn't work, and the Dispute Resolution Manager from the Flood Zone Determination Services emailed Aurelia back and complained that he needed actual numbers, not some crudely drawn shapes. Thinking fast, since everyone was asking me for this and not the builder, I used a landscaping software that I had purchased, loaded the flood map into the system, and drew the house on the lot. Conveniently, it added distances to various objects, and it looked pretty professional, considering the amateur (me) that put it together. Off that went to the flood guy with the fancy title, who apparently found it satisfactory. Score another point for my quick-thinking genius!

Chapter 18

In late July I finally met my builder in person. I had been working with LuMa Construction since May, but I had never actually met Manius or his partner Lucius. I had enough time in my work schedule to take leave and travel down to Norfolk to meet them. I was excited to finally meet the guy that had snatched my house project from the jaws of defeat and helped me carry it across the goal line. Despite the setbacks, we were approaching a closing date, and in my mind, once we closed on the mortgage, Manius could do his magic and I'd have a beautiful house.

As I was planning my trip, Tatiana called me with a complaint. Manius hadn't filled out the forms for his Union Mortgage builder application, and he hadn't finished the VA builder application. To build a home on a VA loan requires you to be a VA builder, which requires...you guessed it, another form. I called Manius, and I got a different story. He told me he filled out every form that Tatiana sent, only to receive yet more forms or requests for information. He also sounded extremely frustrated.

I quickly realized I was in a bit of a pickle. As the customer, normally I wouldn't care about disputes between the builder and the mortgage company. They would just sort of handle themselves. But because these two groups had never worked with each other, the only common ground they had was me. As the common ground, I had to settle disputes, without angering either the people providing me with the hundreds of thousands of dollars required to build a house, or the people taking those hundreds of thousands of dollars and turning them into a house.

"Good times!", I thought. If I wanted my dream house, I would have to find a way to make it work. I decided to pray to Saint Rebecca for some guidance. Catholics define a Saint as someone that has passed away and the Church recognizes is in Heaven. Most of the time, we think of Saints as famous people, such as Saint Theresa or Saint Francis. Those people are venerated as Saints because they lived noble lives and have at least two associated miracles attributed to them. This bar is a bit high, because miracle attribution requires the Catholic Church verify you only prayed to that particular person that wasn't quite a Saint yet, and that the miracle is indeed a miracle and couldn't have naturally happened on its own. By the way, fun fact, when they hold meetings to discuss whether someone should be venerated as a Saint, there is actually a person called the Devil's Advocate who has to argue against them to help shake out any missing details. Because my Rebecca died early, she never had a chance to sin, and because we had baptized and Confirmed her in the Catholic Church, she got a one-way ticket to Heaven. So, while I had plenty of Saints to pick from, I figured I'd have the undivided attention of Saint Rebecca when it came to my little housing issues.

Sure enough, after a bit of prayer, the answer came to me. I called Tatiana back and told her since I was traveling to see Manius anyway, could we all perhaps have a phone conference when I got there? She agreed, Manius agreed, and I agreed.

After driving through New York City, my path to the Norfolk area goes through Delaware and Virginia's Eastern Shore. It's pretty quiet, unassuming farm country, without much to look at. It gave me plenty of alone time, and I can only listen to so much music, so I used that time to talk to Saint Rebecca. If you're wondering, no booming voice came back in response to my prayers, or much of anything for that matter. I just talked openly about my frustrations, especially about the things that I thought should just work, but apparently didn't, without a lot of effort on my part. After I finished complaining, I asked for help with the upcoming meeting, to receive guidance on what to say and when to say it. In the middle of the Chesapeake Bay Bridge Tunnel, I took a moment to appreciate that I was so far out in the water that I couldn't see land on either side. Despite this, I knew that I would arrive on the other side, that I would in fact make landfall again. After my long prayer, I felt better, a bit stronger, and ready to take on the challenges.

After spending the night at Chris' house, I drove to Manius' office space and met him for the first time. Manius was tall, blond and in-shape. At some point in our conversations, he had told me he owned a CrossFit gym, so between that and building homes, he probably couldn't afford to be unhealthy. His office was a small rented space in an industrial strip mall, ironically not far from where I purchased my first townhouse twelve years earlier.

We had a bit of time before our phone call and I saw a printed copy of the extensive PowerPoint presentation that I had made, so we reviewed it together. Room by room we perused the details. It really helped to have it organized, since I had forgotten some of the details until I saw them again on paper. You don't realize how many little details there are in a home until you have to tell someone else how to build that home. Any particular room will have a wall color, door style, trim, lighting, floor type, ceiling color, window type and location, and where any outlets are located. Bathrooms and the kitchen have more fixtures, each of which has a specific style.

Speaking of fixtures, Manius pulled out the VA home application. "I've never seen this form before, can you help me fill it out?" he asked me, to which I agreed. We walked through the form, and the amount of detail requested was a bit stunning. The VA wanted information on every single fixture in the house, down to the model number and style. For example, in the guest bathroom, the sink faucet was a model T6620, the towel bar was model YB2218, and the toilet paper holder was a model YB2208. Yes, the VA was extremely concerned with the brand and model of the small piece of molded metal that my toilet paper spun off of! Manius said he had never been asked for this level of detail before. Perhaps it was fate that brought us together, since most people wouldn't have been able to provide that level of detail.

Soon it was time for the phone call, so I called Tatiana and then conferenced in Vance and Aurelia from my cell phone. I had asked Manius to start, so he detailed the forms he had filled out, and then asked a few questions. Tatiana went through the forms, and between her, me and Manius, we spent about fifteen minutes on form details. Everything seemed to be progressing well. Questions were receiving straightforward answers, and clarity arrived like a fog lifting with the sun. I then discussed our way forward and timeframe. Manius would send documents after this meeting, Tatiana would process these documents and would send them to the appraiser. "Is there any reason we can't send these to the appraiser today?" I asked.

"Well, I don't have everything I need." Tatiana replied. Darkness set in, and I stared dumbfounded at Manius, who quietly mouthed "See, I told you," with a grimace on his face. "Ok Tatiana," I calmly retorted, "I'm not smart on this stuff, can you walk me through what else you need?" Sure enough, Tatiana had some other information she needed for a form, which Manius agreed to provide. Then the moment I had prayed and practiced for came. I announced to our small group "Tatiana, can you walk everyone through what happens from now until we get the appraisal back and close the loan."

Tatiana meticulously walked everyone through the steps. Manius and I occasionally interrupted her to ask for more details on specific areas. It was important that she, and not I, describe the details so that it was her plan being described. What had been happening, much to everyone's frustration, was that each organization was on the "last house" plan, but everyone's "last house" was different. Manius' last house didn't involve a VA loan or working with Union Mortgage. Tatiana's last house probably involved a builder like Manicured Homes where they had a pre-existing relationship. This put everyone at odds with each other. Tatiana describing the ultimate plan in detail, and Manius agreeing to it, meant we all finally got on the same page.

Before hanging up the phone, we set a tentative closing date of August 28. I was feeling pretty marvelous, having solved some problems and brought us all together. We ordered a survey and appraisal, Manius finished up his VA forms, and I drove back to Chris' house with a smile on my face.

Chapter 19
August 2017

The survey results came back on the 7th of August, and there were no surprises. The survey listed my property as exactly 3.548 acres, and showed the exact locations of pins and survey markers. A drainage ditch made one of the long borders, and the street made another. The back and one side were not as easy to see, and the dark impenetrable forest meant there wasn't always a clear delineation where one property ended and another began.

That next week Manius called. The VA assessor had called him looking for the house, and was apparently surprised that there wasn't a home on the property. Manius had sent him the survey, house diagram and an approximation of where the house would be located. After explaining that this was a new home construction, as previously indicated on the meticulously filled out forms, he finally was satisfied and replied that he would finish the assessment.

I had considered becoming a real estate assessor at one time. I figured I could let my kids conduct the assessments and I would get rich easily, since at no time had an assessor ever delighted me with their brilliance or intellect. Maybe that's a bit harsh, and maybe there are really sharp assessors out there, but if so, I haven't encountered them. Most assessments consist of someone finding three recently sold homes that are similar to the house being assessed. You then compensate for any differences, slap a percentage up or down based on the current market trend, and call it a properly conducted assessment. Given the expansion of the internet, my kids could do that from my laptop with a Zillow login and maybe thirty minutes of free time. I had already looked at Zillow and made sure the price for the home matched what an assessment would find.

Closing was still scheduled for the 28th of August, so I was constantly emailing or calling Vance and Tatiana. Departing work one day, I saw an email from Vance saying the assessment was in and we should talk on the phone. "Success" I thought! I returned home, changed out of my uniform, and gave him a call.

> *"Ryan, the assessment came in forty-five thousand dollars too low."*

I recoiled in shock. "How?" I asked. That didn't make any sense to me. Vance sent me the assessment, and I immediately reviewed the comparison section. Sure enough, none of the homes used for comparison were direct matches. That part wasn't a surprise. The compensations to account for the differences did surprise me. All the homes were nearly 1,000 square feet less than mine, but the compensation for square footage was only fifty dollars a square foot.

That made no sense. Homes in a given area tend to hover around a certain price per square foot, which was an easy way to compare them. For example, in that area well-built homes were around 130 dollars a square foot. If you saw a home priced at 150 dollars a square foot, it needed to be premium quality or else it was probably a lousy deal. Any Zillow search easily confirms this, and it's not uncommon for a real estate agent to use this fact when working with clients.

But that wasn't the worst part. The compensation homes were all on small, quarter of an acre lots that are typical for suburban America. My lot was three and a half acres. We weren't living in farm land, where acreage is cheap. The three and a quarter acre difference was easily worth 120 to 150 thousand dollars. A real estate investor could carve my property into twelve to fourteen homes. Yet there was no compensation for lot size. None whatsoever. I thought I was looking at a common core math problem, and in this magical math land somehow 0.25 acres is the same as 3.548 acres.

"Obviously this is wrong," I told Vance on the phone, "so how do we fight this." Vance sounded glum. "It's the VA, they don't change assessments. In fact, I've never seen it before."

That was the death knell. I had read the same stories in my research. VA assessors had a bad rap. It wasn't hard to find internet tales of VA assessors telling military families to find extra money or else they couldn't buy a home. When I purchased my first home, I was specifically warned away from using a VA loan for exactly that reason. Worse still, after the economic crash in 2008, VA assessors had gotten even more stringent.

I asked Vance for some time to do research. I then called Nadine and explained the situation. Rather than hopelessness, Nadine reacted in pure anger, especially when I listed the compensation addresses and amounts. "I appreciate your sentiment, but what can I do?" I asked. "You contest it, of course!" she told me without hesitation. "He's obviously wrong. Get a list of better addresses and I'll call him."

"You can contest the assessment?" I asked, a bit stunned.

"Sure," Nadine replied, "You just send a better list of addresses."

How, in all my research, had I not found this? I was dumbstruck. I figured short of clerical errors I was hosed. Energized by that piece of knowledge, I thanked her and dove into the task of finding better compensations. Sure enough, soon I had a list of eight homes, which after re-consulting with Nadine, I whittled down to the best three homes and submitted to Vance.

Nadine called me later to say she had "called the assessor" and he had "agreed to reconsider his assessment." The way she said it, in a cold, professional manner, reminded me of a mobster that took the contract to empty your garbage and you did not ask about what other sort of business they engaged in. It sounded like Nadine had cornered the assessor and threatened him with a lead pipe, and if he didn't cooperate, he might come away missing a finger or wearing cement shoes. I'm sure nothing of this sort happened, and

I would never, ever research any of these obviously false allegations, nor would I check my garbage can in the future for bodies.

I had totally misjudged Nadine. Every real estate agent I had worked with in the past had been mediocre at best, and in plenty of cases just sucked. Nadine was older and wiser. She had played this game before, and she knew all the secret moves. She was the little old lady that busts out ju jitsu on a would-be petty thief in the 7-11 at two in the morning. Or the mobster's secretary that turns out to be the real brains of the organization. Something like that. I'm still not checking my garbage cans.

I submitted new compensation homes to Vance that day. Two weeks later, the assessor sent a letter agreeing to change his assessment, and it came out to the exact amount we needed to close on the house. He also wrote in a separate email that he would not be checking his garbage for bodies and kindly asked that no horse heads be placed in his bed. I'm obviously joking about the last part, because I don't even know the assessors name and it's all just a business deal anyway. Plus, I wouldn't want any emotional attachment to someone that got on Nadine's bad side.

Chapter 20
September 2017

Aurelia and Cassia worked closing documents, and Cassia called me to say she could close on September 11. For military members, September 11 clearly marks the transition from a post-Cold War mindset to a War on Terror mindset. On September 11, 2001, I was still in college, and that morning I was working as a computer administrator in a small office on the engineering campus. My phone rang, and it was my boss' mom trying to find him. She expressed concern that "someone just flew a plane into a building." I thought she was crazy, but I replied that I'd go find him. I walked upstairs, and everyone was clustered around a TV, where I watched in horror as the second plane flew into the World Trade Center. Sixteen years later and that memory is still crystal clear in my brain.

Because Union Mortgage was located in Virginia, I figured they would send a notary to my home for closing. Nope! Cassia informed me I had to drive to Union's office in Mechanicsville, VA to sign documents. That really sucked for me, since I lived eight hours away. Luckily, my brother-in-law Mark lived in nearby Richmond, VA, so I worked out the plan to drive down, sign forms, sleep on his couch, and then drive back the next morning. Despite being 2017, my life was still very much controlled by ink signatures on a rolled piece of tree fiber.

I drove down early that Monday morning, beating the New York City traffic and the inevitable visitors to Ground Zero on that day. The drive was relatively uneventful, but that much time alone was always dangerous for me, since I tend to focus on somber thoughts. Instead, I focused on uplifting memories, like my journey to find a properly sized bath tub for my master bathroom.

Bath tubs and I don't normally mix. I'm over six feet tall, and I barely fit in the standard sized bath tub/shower combination you find in most homes and all cheap hotels. Worse still, that style tub has an overflow protection, so you don't really soak much more than your legs and maybe the upper part of your hips. If you sink any lower, you slosh all that nice hot water out the overflow drain. When Otto asked about a master bathroom bath tub, I told him I needed to find one that fit me, or else we wouldn't have a tub at all.

I started my quest at the local bathroom warehouse that had a decent sized showroom. I walked in cleanly dressed and proceeded to jump into tub after tub after tub. Like Goldilocks sampling ursine breakfast, I found reasons to dislike all the bath tubs. Unlike Goldilocks, none of the tubs were "just right" for me. I did some internet research and discovered that Fergusons, a huge bath store, had its headquarters in Newport News, VA, and when I drove up to its massive studio, I smiled. This place, I thought, would have my tub.

It did not. I must have jumped in and out of a hundred tubs. I tried darn near every sizable tub in the store, and the store was massive. Defeated, I tried two other smaller stores down the street. No such luck. Nothing was "just right." Most tubs weren't long enough. The tubs that were long enough had weird slanted angles where you were supposed to sit at. They looked pretty in a showroom, but were entirely impractical for the purpose of sitting and relaxing. I left the last store wishing that bath tub designers would take a note from hot tub makers, who built molded, comfortable seats you never wanted to leave.

My store frustrations forced me into internet research. I found a website where I could enter measurements as a filter, which helped me filter out short tubs that were never going to hit the mark. As I reviewed the results, I recognized many of the tubs I had already sat in. Discarding them, the remaining list of tubs was pretty small. Soon, I found a tub that had potential, made by the manufacturer MAAX, which seemed to design more practical tubs. The model, the Crescendo, had the right length and a back that was inclined so you could relax into the tub. Even better, the overflow was located high up, so you could actually soak more than your legs.

There was one problem: nobody had this tub. I called places all along the I-95 corridor, but nobody had it. Then, I found a large bath store in northern Connecticut that told me on the phone they had one on the display floor. Their store was not on the way to anything. I decided I would loop it into the tail end of a trip to Norfolk to see the builder. After ten hours of driving from Norfolk, I headed further north than normal and pulled into the parking lot of this bath store, which for the record was really out in the middle of nowhere. I walked in to find the one store employee on the phone, and the store was otherwise a ghost town. A bit of wandering and I discovered the tub. I jumped in and...perfection! Right length, right depth, and comfortable to boot! I snapped a selfie and a picture of the display model number and continued my journey home.

Those positive memories kept me going while I drove down to Mechanicsville. I made it to a small office building where I met Cassia for the first time. I still find it weird to have worked with someone on something so important, yet have never met them in real life. Cassia brought me a stack of paperwork, and as I typically do, I read nearly everything, so the closing took about an hour. It's a lot of paperwork, but I read it to compare it to what I had been sent before, and I asked about the differences.

One that stuck out to me was the loan type. When a VA construction to permit loan closes, the initial loan isn't a VA loan, since the VA doesn't do interest only loans. You sign paperwork at a VA closing for a conventional loan, then check that the VA paperwork for the final loan rollover is accurate. I had already sent in changes for the VA paperwork earlier that were reflected on the final documents.

I had also wired over a lot of money to finish closing. While the VA allows you to put no money down, you still have closing costs and other fees. I had saved this money up over time by setting aside special pays from the Navy. Remember that Cost of Living Allowance, or COLA, I received because everything is expensive in Hawaii? Just electricity alone is forty-one cents a kilowatt hour, vice eight to ten cents in most other states. Food is the same way. But for my family, living on base housing saved us on the electrical bill, and religiously shopping at the commissary saved our food bill. This money, stashed away in a mutual fund until recently, covered my closing costs and other fees.

My hour with Cassia wore out a pen's worth of ink while signing documents, but then it was done. I had closed a VA loan, despite firing a builder, cornering a VA assessor and living in another state. I left triumphant. Now we could start actually building the house. That's the fun part, to watch my design go up and become something real. Forever home was finally moving out of the dream world and into the real world.

Chapter 21
October 2017

The fun part of home building finally began with kitchen cabinet designs. Up until this point, the YouTube, Internet and library research I was performing largely consisted of me doing the research and relaying that information to my wife. Rachel would nod and sometimes show excitement, but she just didn't care about roofing shingles, encapsulated crawl spaces or Zip system sheathing the way I did.

When I asked her about kitchen cabinets though, Rachel was all in. She had lots of opinions because that was her space and she could be quite particular when she wanted to be. Quickly she found that it was a daunting task to take a blank space and draw in your kitchen, so to help her, I drew out the kitchen space and cut out paper pieces sized for the refrigerator, stove and dishwasher. I had also snagged some Delta and Moen catalogs, which had lots of pictures of various kitchen designs to help keep her creative juices flowing.

We did hit a snag at first when it came to our upper cabinets. We had requested nine-foot ceilings on the first floor (normal ceilings are eight feet tall). The height was better for Christmas trees, decorations and hanging things on a larger wall. The problem was that anything in a cabinet nearly nine feet up was difficult to reach without a step ladder. I argued that the top cabinets should have a glass or plexiglass front and be lit from inside, so that you can display objects in them. I remembered Rachel's nice-looking plates and other kitchen decorations that normally hid inside the cabinets most of the year. Why not put them on display, I argued, so that guests could enjoy them?

Rachel was hesitant. She just couldn't see the usefulness in that. I tried to compare it to the passage in the book of Matthew where Jesus implores people to not hide their talents, because "neither do men light a candle and put it under a bushel, but on a candlestick, and it giveth light unto all that are in the house." "That passage describes our cabinets exactly" I explained. Eventually, I persuaded Rachel to give it a go.

We gathered Rachel's ideas onto paper, building a large list of requirements that the kitchen must have. I'm not an artist, but I stayed at a Holiday Inn once, so I took out my non-magical pencil and scratched away on a few sheets of paper to illustrate what cabinets went where, approximate sizes and what cabinet hardware paired with each drawer. The final drawing resembled something a 4th grader would sketch out. Actually, the 4th grader's artwork would look better. My chicken scratch appears to have barely graduated Kindergarten, but for the purposes of getting something on paper, it was good enough.

Rachel was particular about drawer sizing for pots. Most people have a few vertical cabinets where pots are shoved in, which results in constant complete cabinet unloading to reach that one particular pot in the back of the cabinet. Other people have a cool hanging rack where all the pots hang in the air over the kitchen island as tempting targets for children armed with Nerf guns. Rachel wasn't a fan of either option. She wanted large pullout drawers that were deep enough to support jumbo-sized pots. That meant two large, wide, deep drawers in the kitchen island that were able to store nearly all our pots. Cabinet unloading and Nerf gun targeting not required.

We scanned my Kindergarten-level artwork and sent it to Manius. Manius indicated he was going to try a different cabinet maker based out of North Carolina. He could always use his current guy, but "sometimes he's a bit slow," so it would be smart to have alternatives. After two weeks, the cabinet folks said they wanted to meet, so I took some time off and drove down to Norfolk to meet them.

Along the way I stopped by Shade and Shutter Systems in Branford, CT, right off the I-95 freeway. I had been looking into ways to make the new house more secure, and stumbled upon a video of a screen door that a rather large man could not kick through. Intrigued, I realized the company that made the screens was in Connecticut, so I called them and scheduled a visit to see their screen door. They also made shutter systems that rolled down to protect windows from hurricane-force winds. That was particularly important to me since Virginia was occasionally bombarded by hurricanes, and I wanted the house to survive unscathed.

True to the video, Shade and Shutter had a screen door setup. They handed me a sledge hammer and with a smile told me to "go nuts." So, I went nuts. I had some residual anger, so I let it loose on the screen door. True to the video, and to my amazement, the door held up. I gave the sales rep a copy of my house plan, which had the door measurements, so that he could provide a quote. Walking out of the store, I returned to my journey south to meet the cabinet maker.

The new cabinet maker sent three people to meet with me. They had taken my kindergarten art submission and mocked up the entire kitchen in a three-dimensional drawing. It was impressive! Up until that point, it had been difficult to visualize the kitchen from a bunch of flat floorplan drawings, but now in three dimensions the layout became crystal clear. I was familiar with 3D software, but hadn't placed a lot of value on it until that moment.

We talked through every drawer. Yes, every drawer. Needless to say, we talked a lot, because there were a lot of drawers to talk about. We covered every single drawer hardware pullout. That was particularly important because corners have a tendency to waste space in the back, where you can't reach items. To avoid that, we laid out the lazy Susan spinners and pullouts to use that space. We also had a pullout trash and recycling combination, with a trash can large enough for a family. My mom had a pullout trash can, which worked for her and my dad, but was way too small for a family, and I had learned that lesson the hard way after we visited their home a few times.

I made one change to keep costs down. The corner where the bar meets the kitchen had a rounded counter top and cabinet. The cabinet maker cautioned that while he could make a round door, it was challenging and expensive. I didn't care all that much, so I had him cut the corner at a diagonal and put in a flat door. My reasoning was that I would only keep expensive things that I or Rachel were really passionate about. For example, I wouldn't sacrifice the encapsulated crawl space, because I really cared about it. But a rounded cabinet? Not worth fighting over.

I left that meeting upbeat and excited. I knew what my kitchen would look like, and I was pretty confident that the cabinet maker had all the little details I wanted captured. About two weeks later, Manius sent me the quote from the cabinet maker. It was five pages long. Page one was a company cover page. Page two talked about the cabinet makers history. Page three was a quality page, describing the wood used for the cabinets in great detail. Page four had almost no information except a line that declared "Estimate: $95,000." Page five was another company logo page.

I thought 95,000 dollars sounded like a lot of money, but I'm not a cabinet guy, so I asked Manius. Sure enough, it was more than double what he was expecting. I think the cabinet people "went nuts" on the quote. For some reason they thought I was a high roller that just had bags of money sitting around. About the same time, I got the quote from Shade and Shutter for $35,000. Granted, that covered every door and window, and I really liked their product, but I also didn't have bags of money sitting around. Manius took care of sending all the information to his normal cabinet guy, and I thanked Shade and Shutter for sending me a quote. Both meetings were slightly disappointing, but I had no reason to think we were off-track.

Chapter 22
December 2017

The rest of 2017 was fairly uneventful. I emailed Manius about two items: the water heater and ethernet cabling for cameras. I had done a fair amount of research on water heaters, and I wanted a hybrid water heater. Normally, water heaters were heated by either natural gas or electricity, and you simply looked for well-designed insulation and tank capacity. But there was a third type that not many people talked about. The hybrid water heater is an electric heater that has an air-sourced heat pump on the top. The heat pump sucks in hot air from the room the water heater is in and runs that air over a set of coils. The heat from the air is used to heat the water, and the unit exhausts cool air.

Southeast Virginia is hot in the summer. We're talking nasty, 100+ degree heat index hot with humidity to boot. There was no way I was going to work in my garage without some way of cooling it. The hybrid water heater would do just that, and it would use that hot air from the garage to heat my shower. It was a win-win. Manius had never installed one before, so I gave him the model and manufacturer to help him figure out how to install it correctly.

I also asked Manius to have the electrician route ethernet cables to every room and to outside the house for cameras. Ethernet cables are networking cables made of twisted pairs of wires that send data at really high rates, much faster than what you can send wirelessly. Even better, some network switches could send small amounts of power over the ethernet cable to power devices. Power over ethernet, or PoE, could let you power and hook up a security camera, or a light, or even a speaker. Since it was easy to route cables while the house was being built, I picked the sites where I wanted ethernet in the house. For the electrician, it was simply another cable, so it wasn't hard for him to do while he was moving cables for everything else.

December came and Manius wanted to start clearing trees. I had wanted to start earlier, but he was finishing other projects and reassured me it wouldn't delay the house at all. The problem was that clearing wasn't included in the price. We needed to clear about three-quarters of an acre of the front part of the property, plus bring in a lot of sand and soil to build the pad that the house would sit on. The sand is important because you want water to drain away from the house and foundation. Virginia has notoriously sticky clay soil that loves to hold onto water and takes forever to dry out. That moisture being plastered against your foundation would eventually cause cracks and rot wood. Encapsulating the crawl space helps prevent that, but not having the water there in the first place also helps.

Clearing and sand was 10,000 dollars. When I said I saved up a lot of money, I wasn't kidding, but closing costs had bitten into our funding a bit. Thankfully, my wife, or rather, my wife's parents, bailed us out. Her parents had saved money for each of their kids, but Rachel had never spent it, since we got married right when she graduated school and we didn't need to spend it on anything. Well, now we needed help, and I was extremely grateful that Rachel's mom and dad were willing to help us.

I did save a bit of money by asking Manius' partner, Lucius, to cut the trees into eight-foot sections and leave them on the property. I planned to cut them up into firewood later, and I thought it was dumb to pay to have them taken to a landfill, especially since I would have a wood burning fireplace.

I stopped by in early December, and no clearing had happened yet. I walked in the forest on the property and wondered how it would turn from blank land into my home in only a few months. I had finally received orders to leave Connecticut in June. While we had enjoyed our time in Connecticut, it was never going to be our final home. Part of my trip in December involved talking with a funeral home about transferring Rebecca from her donated grave in Connecticut to a more suitable location in Virginia. After some internet research, I spent a day driving to five different cemeteries, seeing how far each was from the house and whether it would be nice to spend any time there. One of the cemeteries was essentially an open field under high power electric lines. Not only was it kind of uninviting, but the lack of shade would preclude visiting in the summer. Luckily, one of the other cemeteries was relatively close, had a nice setup and had at least a few trees for shade.

I had contacted the funeral home that ran the cemetery, only to receive no return phone call. Time and again, I had called, and when someone actually answered the phone, they promised to call me back, only to not do so. That was really frustrating, so I physically stopped by in December. The funeral home employee was surprised to see me, as I guessed he didn't receive too many drop-in visits. We discussed how to do a transfer, and I gave him our local funeral home's number so they could start the process. Relieved to finally solve that problem, I drove to the house for one more task.

I had always wanted to have my own orchard. I had dreamed of walking around my property, picking off apples, mulberries, and even more rare fruit like pawpaw. In Hawaii, we had about ten large mango trees around us that just dumped mangos everywhere. I would spend afternoons with the kids gathering baskets of mangos to bring back to the house. The nicely shaped mangos would become breakfast fruit. The bruised ones would be skinned and blended, then poured onto a drying sheet and dehydrated into fruit leather. It was about the healthiest snack you could have, with no preservatives or other additives, just blended, dried mango.

Unless I was lucky though, military life and its constant moving meant trying to grow fruit trees was a fruitless endeavor. It was a lot of work to plant, water and establish a tree in any particular area, let alone an orchard of trees. Now things were different. I did need to figure out how good or bad my soil was, and the local agricultural extension recommended sending a soil sample for testing. I swung by their office and grabbed three small carboard boxes, which I took to the property. I measured and dug samples in what would be the front yard, side yard and backyard, placing the soil in a Ziplock bag and then into each little box. After labeling each box, I drove back to the extension and saved myself the postage by handing it directly to the extension employee. Then it was back on the road, returning to Connecticut to celebrate one last Christmas in our rented home.

Chapter 23

The new year rang in with the sounds of chainsaws dropping the giant pine trees in what would become my front yard. One by one, these trees, most of which were three or four feet across, came down with a crash. Lucius was quite skilled with the chainsaw, and after cutting the trees into eight-foot chunks he stacked them with an excavator away from the jobsite.

Because my house would be so far back from the road, Manius suggested installing a crushed concrete driveway. This uses recycled concrete broken into small pieces and used in place of gravel or poured concrete. Gravel driveways tend to be expensive, and poured concrete even more so. I considered having an asphalt driveway, but my dad talked me out of it on a phone call. "Don't forget that Virginia is hot, and you'll be baking on your driveway." Good point, I thought, so the crushed concrete stayed.

Manius mentioned that they used a geotextile fabric when they installed the driveway. My inner geek demanded satisfaction, so I started researching the fabric. Turns out that geotextile fabric reduced soil movement when large vehicles drove on top of it. I even managed to find a research paper that showed fabric rolls on sandy beaches allowed amphibious vehicles to unload tanks. My dad, a retired Marine, wasn't surprised.

The house layout presented a small driveway problem. There was a deep ditch in front of the house with two existing culverts that were the natural choice to put the driveway over. However, one was wedged between a power pole and a fire hydrant. We would have to move one of those to make the space wide enough for a vehicle. The other culvert was on the side closer to the neighborhood. Having my garage open to the neighborhood didn't look right, so we flipped the house to have the garage open to the nearby woods.

This required a really long driveway. I originally wanted a U-shaped driveway. While a bit more expensive, it would make it easy to turn around. Rachel wasn't a fan. Between the two of us, she's the thriftier one. She didn't think we would need that U-shape. After arguing back and forth, we agreed on an S-shaped driveway that came in on one side, crossed in front of the house, and then connected to the garage.

Laying out the driveway helped me focus on the overall property design. I had considerable plans for my homestead. I imagined adding a garden, a few ducks, a shed and eventually a small chapel. My friend Chris had put a chapel on their property, which gave him a place to retreat to and pray away from the house. While I worked with the funeral home on Rebecca's internment, I learned the cemetery only used bronze plates to mark graves in the infant section. This meant the large grave stone we had purchased was no longer needed. I wasn't giving the stone up (it's expensive), and I couldn't throw it away, so I wanted an appropriate place for it. A backyard chapel was perfect.

This homestead plotting also educated me on zoning rules. I learned about different residential zoning and what it allowed, or didn't allow. My property was zoned for R-15. The zoning defined how close you could build to the edge of the property, what kinds of out buildings you could have, and whether you could have animals, and what type of animals, on the property. My research turned up a few surprises. For example, there is an entire section about keeping Vietnamese Potbellied Pigs. No kidding. Apparently, the Vietnamese Potbellied Pigs have some sort of lobby group, because they have carved out an exception that allows them to not be viewed as livestock. You can keep one as a pet with a permit, provided you don't slaughter the animal on property, it stays under 120 pounds, is housed inside and is vaccinated.

While R-15 didn't stop me from what I wanted to do, I saw that RE-1, the residential estate zoning, was a better fit. It was designed for lots at least three acres large. It allowed more farm animals and more variety. I asked Manius if rezoning the property would stop work, and he replied that it would not. I created an eBuild account on the city's website, filed the necessary paperwork, paid my fee and submitted.

The city called me a day later with some follow-up questions. Apparently, I was the first rezoning request for 2018, and they didn't receive many residents placing requests. The city employee on the phone sounded nice, told me that everything was in order, and that I should expect a decision by the end of January. I asked if I needed to attend the meeting, but he assured me I didn't.

It felt like a Staples Commercial with the 'Easy' button. I hung up the phone and thought, "Wow, that was easy."

Turns out, it wasn't. The city zoning board rejected my proposal. Apparently, they didn't understand why I was doing it, and since I wasn't there to talk to it, it was rejected. Mercifully, they sent my application fee back. Lesson learned for dealing with City Hall: if you're not there in person, don't expect anything to be easy.

Chapter 24
April 2018

I spent most of the rest of the winter in Connecticut, but in April I managed to travel to Norfolk for a work trip. The Groton detachment that I was in charge of reported to a Navy Captain in Norfolk. In April that changed, and suddenly I reported to a Navy Captain in Georgia. My detachment also grew and took over another shop in the Norfolk area. Now I was a detachment to a Georgia command, and as a detachment, I had a detachment in Norfolk. If that sounds confusing, it was. The Georgia Captain, Captain Count (not to be confused with the Sesame Street character) wanted to see what he was taking over, so I agreed to meet him in Norfolk. We had a few long days of work, since the portion of the Norfolk command had a lot of issues to resolve.

At the end of one of the days, my new Captain asked "Hey, how's your house coming along?" I hadn't heard anything from Manius in a while, except that there was some issue with the city requiring a silt fence while the land was being cleared. There was still enough daylight, so I offered to drive out to the site, since I had driven my own vehicle down. We loaded up interested parties and drove out. Along the way one of the guys described the process he journeyed on to build his house in Georgia. It took him about a year, and because his time frame was more flexible, he was better able to control costs. We exchanged some notes and I relayed the struggles I had building this house. "Thankfully that's all over now," I declared.

We pulled up to...a very blank piece of land.

Captain Count asked "So when are you expecting to move in?" I responded "July sir." He shook his head a bit "I hate to tell you, but I don't think that's going to happen."

Later that night, I wrote Manius an email asking if we were on track. His reply was "We might not be ready by July."

I sat stunned in my hotel room. This whole time, I had trusted Manius to keep the project on track. I had made monthly interest-only payments on the land, with the hope that it would all stop in July so I could stop draining money needlessly on the house. Now here I was, in April, getting ready to leave my command at the end of June, and I had no home to move into, and more importantly, no backup plan.

I wanted to scream. I felt cheated again. I had done all this work, only to have my hopes thrown against the wall and shattered like a cheap light bulb. Manius didn't even have the courtesy to tell me that things weren't going well earlier, which would have given me time to build a backup plan. Was he incompetent? Overwhelmed? I didn't know, and the end result was the same.

I briefly considered firing him. Then I looked back at my notes. Who would I hire, I thought? Everyone else had come out more expensive.

Others had never written back. If I fired him, the loan would collapse, and I'd still owe payments on the land. Finding a new builder would be difficult. If I didn't find one, I'd have spent all this money for nothing. At that point, it became clear to me that I would either make it to the end of this journey with Manius and Lucius, or we would all fail together.

That's the reality check that you won't get from your friends that have never built homes. Years later, people would tell me I should have fired LuMa Construction, or charged them extra. It's on a long list of things that people who have never built a custom house tell you to do, but that they really have no clue about. Sure, in a perfect world, you would have another builder lined up, salivating at the prospect of building your house. But the world isn't perfect. If you had a better builder, you would have picked them by the time you got to closing. Since you probably don't build many homes, you're picking someone you've never worked with and hoping for the best, and as I discovered, even five-star reviews by customers, the BBB and the local building commission don't necessarily translate to future success.

And charging more or suing someone? Sure, you can try to do that, and you might win some money. Maybe. A builder contract has an awful lot of clauses for weather, city delays, and other things. Are you a lawyer and can successfully persuade a judge to overlook those clauses? If so, you probably have enough money to pay one of the more expensive builders that have bigger, designated crews and can build on a timeline. Suing a builder is difficult, expensive, and even if you win, you don't have a house in the end, just some smug satisfaction that you were right, which doesn't protect you from the rain.

The cold reality is that once you sign a contract, you're stuck with the builder until it's over. Buckle up for the long and bumpy ride, or don't step into the car in the first place. Maybe that's not what you see on HGTV, but that's reality.

When I returned to Connecticut, after breaking the news to Rachel, and dealing with the accompanying shock, we sat down and built a plan. We needed a place to live for a few months, so the lease had to be short. Now, I bet a bunch of you backseat lawyers reading this are going to say "Well, why not just invoke the Sailors and Soldiers Act clause and break a lease?" I did in fact read the Sailors and Soldiers Act. For people not familiar with this law, it allows military members to break leases and other contracts without penalty due to military orders. Guess what? It requires a new set of orders that move you out of the area. Since I would have already executed orders to move to the area, I wouldn't have a set of orders that required me to move. Now, I'm betting if I simply asked, I might be allowed to break a contract, but I wasn't willing to take that risk.

We found apartments that gave three- and six-month leases. I chose a three-month lease option because Manius promised me he'd be done "before Halloween." That significantly narrowed our options, as most apartments don't even consider three-month leases. We ended up with only three viable options at that point. Rachel then called one of our friends in the area and asked her to drive by each of the places and put "eyes on" the apartment buildings. Her description of one place was "pretty old and tired," so we had a hard pass on that one. In the end, we settled on The Amber Apartments. It seemed like a nice place, was somewhat close to school, was close to work and the house, and had enough nearby places to walk to for food. Plus, as a bonus, it was across the street from the library. My kids devour books, so that was the perfect distraction while we waited for forever home completion.

The really hard part now was figuring out what things we needed to keep with us while we lived in the apartment, and what would sit in storage while we waited for the house. There was no way all of our stuff would fit in the apartment, and the military wouldn't pay to move our stuff twice. Rachel made a list of all the kitchen equipment we would need, all the clothes we'd have to pack, bedspreads, and a variety of other things. It was more than we'd be able to fit in our vehicle, and we were planning on driving down over two days. "So what do we do now?", I thought, as a I clenched a fist thinking about all the extra steps that Manius was putting me through due to his inability to notify me earlier.

Then it hit me. I would take a few days of leave, drive all our stuff down in a trailer, put it in a storage unit, sign the lease at The Amber, and then fly back and leave my vehicle there. That way, we could all fit in one vehicle on the way down, our stuff would already be there, and we wouldn't have to travel with family and a trailer at the same time. Even better, my son could travel with me to help unload the trailer and spend some quality time together.

I finally had a workable plan. Or so I thought.

S ailors, especially young Sailors, find plenty of ways to derail the best laid plans. I had finished making rental reservations for my trailer and submitting my leave chit over the weekend, and planned to make air reservations later the next day after work. I hadn't been at my desk but ten minutes before my Assistant Officer in Charge stopped by to chat.

> *"Sir, we've got a potential*
> *mast case in Norfolk."*

Captain's Mast, for readers not familiar with the term, is a legal proceeding the military uses to punish minor crimes. It's designed to be quick, efficient, and to "maintain good order and discipline," which really means keep people focused on working and not screwing around. The thinking is, if you quickly stop small crimes, most people will not be tempted to commit larger crimes. It's best compared to traffic court, where the judge can dismiss your charges, fine you or even put you in jail for a limited time, but if you killed someone in a traffic accident, you'd have to go to a different court with a full jury to be sent to jail for a long period of time.

I did not enjoy taking Sailors to Mast. It is not fun to stand in front of a Sailor in a dress uniform and punish them. While in charge, I had ensured that every Mast case I chaired was thorough, and in two cases I punished Sailors in an open forum so that the other Sailors could see the transparency that I used when considering evidence. That kept Sailors focused on following the rules, so I could focus on rewarding instead of punishing Sailors.

I couldn't overlook this case. This Sailor had been assigned to a vessel deployed overseas, and had at one point yelled profanities at the ship's Commanding Officer and disobeyed direct orders. The situation deteriorated so much that the Norfolk detachment had brought him home early and shipped out another Sailor who had not expected to deploy that soon. I then looked at the timeframe to complete the investigation and realized it overlapped with my leave. On top of that, I was running out of time before I would turnover my job to another officer. I did not want to leave open legal matters to someone else to settle.

My Assistant OIC and I worked out a plan. I would drive down and go on leave for the first two days to put my stuff in storage and sign a lease. During that time, I would stay at a friend's house. Then I would transition to government orders, hold the Mast, and then fly back. While on government orders I would stay in a hotel, and I'd pick up my legal officer from the airport. It was a bit convoluted, but we were able to separate what expenses I paid and what expenses the government paid. Once everything was set, we made reservations and all was well. Then I called the airlines and booked a plane ticket for my son that matched mine.

Well before the sun rose, I loaded my son in the car and we headed south. The night before, I had loaded everything I didn't want the movers to touch, plus what we needed for the apartment into the back of the rented trailer. The drive down, now quite familiar to me, was a breeze, and by the time Neil woke up in the backseat, we were already well into New Jersey and away from the New York City traffic. We briefly stopped at Dunkin Donuts before heading over the Chesapeake Bay Bridge Tunnel and into Hampton Roads.

I am not an expert at towing a trailer. Well, I'm not bad at towing a trailer, but I can't back up and park a trailer to save my life. Driving on the freeway doesn't present any problems. When I pulled into Chris' driveway, I had forgotten it was one long, straight driveway, and I would have to back up the trailer to drive back out. We pulled in late in the afternoon, but then I spent the next 15 minutes backing the trailer up in short bursts, jackknifing it twice, but finally getting it turned around and my car facing out.

The next morning was no better. We drove to the storage unit along unusually narrow country roads while trying to keep the trailer from careening off the hitch and into the very deep farm country ditches. As we pulled into town and closer to the storage unit, I realized I had to make a really sharp turn with little open space. The trailer lurched over the curb corner, and I mumbled a short prayer that I hadn't damaged any of my valuables in the back.

Luckily, I didn't stay parked across all three parking spots for too long, since I had made reservations in advance. We drove straight in, unloaded our still unbroken valuables into the storage unit, and locked it up behind us. Loading back into the car, I realized there was no way I was going to back up the trailer, as the units were too close together. Thankfully, after a few minutes of driving around, we found a circular section of driveway large enough for me to turn around. I immediately headed to the U-Haul to turn in the trailer and restore my freedom of movement.

Two days later, after dropping off my son at a friend's place, I put on my dress uniform, picked up my legal officer, and headed to our mast case. I had reviewed the documents before and unfortunately the case was pretty cut and dry. There were multiple eye witnesses claiming that this Sailor had disobeyed orders. I helped setup the small conference room and waited at my podium with three other Sailors. And waited. And waited. After about ten minutes, I asked someone to go check on the Sailor. The Chief (a senior enlisted Sailor) left the room and returned ten minutes later with a sheepish expression on his face.

"Sir, he doesn't have a presentable uniform" I stared back in disbelief. "What do you mean?" I asked. The Chief explained that this Sailor had gained too much weight and couldn't fit into his dress uniform pants, so he purchased new pants from the Navy Exchange, which he then never had hemmed, pressed or cleaned. In fact, the tag might still have been attached, but that was unconfirmed. Thinking on my feet, I replied "He needs to be in 'A' uniform, so get him into 'A' uniform, even if it's a working uniform, and get him in here."

That's a poor start to any legal proceeding, and unfortunately the clown car tragedy continued. Eventually the Sailor entered, a bit disheveled and with an out of regulation haircut and shave. His Chief was embarrassed and offered to send him back, but I waved him off. The proceeding wasn't any better. When I asked him for reasons why he disobeyed the ship's Commanding Officer, he didn't have any. Ultimately, I ended up busting him down a rank and assigning extra duties. More importantly, I spoke with the Chief after about getting him some much-needed life mentoring.

It wasn't long before I was out of my dress uniform, into civilian clothes and at the airport with my son. Leaving my car with a friend, we flew back, confident that we could execute a really solid plan to move to Virginia.

Chapter 26
June 2018

June should have been a straightforward month: move out of my rented house, have movers pack up our goods, turn over my job, and drive south to Virginia. While that might sound overwhelming, it's actually not too bad. My family had moved plenty of times in the past and was used to the craziness that comes with moving.

But then Rachel got sick. I happened to be out of town when she called me, saying she felt dizzy and couldn't see straight. I figured it was a combination of a hotter than normal June, not much air conditioning in our house and the stress of moving out. Rachel insisted on seeing a doctor, but was worried about being able to drive. Not having a lot of options, I called my operations officer, Jarvis, and asked for a favor. Thankfully, he was more than willing to help me out, so he picked up Rachel and took her to the Submarine Base Clinic.

About an hour later Rachel called back laughing. Turns out she was pregnant! That wasn't the funny part though. The nurse walked out, saw my operations officer and congratulated Rachel and Jarvis. Poor Jarvis had to explain to the nurse that he in fact was not the father. Luckily Jarvis has a great sense of humor, and Rachel received much needed medication to help her deal with the first trimester health issues.

Unfortunately, we had more June complications with our kids. Connecticut had a ton of snow fall in December, January and February, and had more school snow days than expected. Because the state requires a certain number of school days, the school year was extended.

To June 26.

Seriously, I'm not joking. That date made my inner child cry great tears of sadness. Who destroys summer break like that? Don't try to hide in the corner, Connecticut Public Schools, you know what you did! To make matters worse, because things can ALWAYS get worse, the school didn't have air conditioning. Now, if you live in the southern United States, this sounds unbelievable, but in the northeast, you can survive using only fans in a classroom just fine, so long as you don't extend the school year into the END OF JUNE!

Anyhow, so the kids were in school while our house was being packed out. They were in school when we moved into the Navy Gateway Inn and Suites, which is the hotel we stayed at before leaving the area. All this, on top of a sick Rachel and me trying to finish all my departing paperwork, made for a bit of a rush in June that I didn't expect. The kids finished school two days before I turned over my command in a large ceremony on the dock near the Historic Ship Nautilus, which is the world's first nuclear power submarine, on display as a museum ship in Groton.

That day was pretty comfortable, with a nice breeze and just enough sun. It wasn't comfortable for Rachel, who put on a smile despite being uncomfortably pregnant. The day was difficult for me too for different reasons. I was turning over a command that had consumed my working life for the last two years. It was tough standing in front of my Sailors and their families, rehashing all the good times while recognizing that it soon wouldn't be mine to command anymore.

The ceremony is pretty straightforward, and at one point I had the opportunity to give a speech. I spoke to the crowd, including almost all of my Sailors, about our last two years together. I talked about the great things we had accomplished, praising the hard work they had done. I didn't gloss over our hard times, including losing Rebecca, but I talked about how despite these challenges, we had come out on top together.

The ceremony ended, we had cake, and then it was weird, because suddenly I was out of a job. I didn't have anything I had to do until the next day. I wasn't going to receive late phone calls from work anymore. I had nothing pressing to do, which isn't normal for me.

The Historic Ship Nautilus has an adjoining museum covering U.S. submarine history, so I wandered around a bit looking at the displays. Most of the displays covered the heroism of submarine Sailors from days past, who overcame severe adversity to pull off some pretty seriously scary operations. In the center of the museum was the battle flag from the *USS BARB* (SS-220). The BARB had fought in World War Two, first supporting the invasion of North Africa, where she sank a Nazi tanker. After she transferred to the Pacific in 1943, she journeyed on what could best be described as a rampage. Not only did she sink a Japanese aircraft carrier, the Un'yo, in 1944, but she would ravage convoys in the East China Sea later that year. Her battle flag had small Japanese flags denoting every vessel that BARB either sank or damaged.

The most unique feature of her flag was the pictures of gun emplacements and a train at the bottom. This denoted the BARB's attack on mainland Japan in July of 1945. BARB's crew, led by Commander Eugene Fluckey, first shelled different Japanese towns with rockets from the submarine, marking the first time a submarine had attacked a land target. Later that month, BARB covertly landed a number of Sailors, who rigged up explosives that derailed a train on the Japanese islands.

You had to admire the Navy for this. After suffering a humiliating attack at Pearl Harbor at the start of the war, then getting routinely trounced in battle after battle with the Japanese Navy for the next six months, they had bounced back with a vengeance. The Navy had two challenges to overcome. The first challenge was the bureaucratic inertia to copy the past. Submarines started the war as little more than scouts, but by the end they had brought Japan to its knees by accounting for over fifty percent of Japanese shipping sunk. In 1945, Japan had to restrict families to one cooking pot, melting down the rest to build airplane spare parts. The second challenge was a human resources problem. In the 1930s, the focus was on keeping submarines from breaking. Submarine commanders grew up in a risk-adverse environment, and in the opening days of World War Two, they didn't take the risks needed to press attacks on Japan. Slowly over the war, these risk-adverse commanders were replaced with young, aggressive commanders that put their submarines in harm's way. While this got many of them killed (submarines suffered a twenty percent casualty rate, the highest in the Navy during the war), this also helped bring the Japanese war machine to a grinding halt and an ultimate end to the war.

When you're in a job for so long, it's easy to forget that you are part of a larger organization with a rich history. Moments like this, where I could simply soak in the enormity of it all, helped me to remember why I signed up for the Navy in the first place. Before I crawled into bed that night, I received an email from Manius. He was trying to make some changes in the plans and was having a hard time reaching Otto, the home designer. I sent Otto a quick email and text message, then turned over to sleep, not thinking too hard about what should be an easy fix.

Washington, DC is a pretty cool place to visit as a tourist. We had made reservations at the Gateway Marriott, which is located right on top of a Metro Station that connected the hotel to all the DC monuments. The Navy allowed two nights of travel before arriving in Norfolk, and we left early enough to spend one and a half days in DC, exploring monuments, the Smithsonian Institute, and eating the occasionally delicious street food. Rachel spent much of that time at the Marriott, surprised at its upscale nature and enjoying the free food and pampering while feeling the ill effects of pregnancy.

Our apartment wasn't ready right away, so we had to spend a few days at the Navy Gateway Inn and Suites in Norfolk. That hotel was located right by the main Navy base, called the Norfolk Naval Station. Navy bases seem to be located in the worst part of any town, and Norfolk Naval Station is no exception. For example, San Diego is a beautiful city, but the Navy base there is located at 32nd Street and its dangerous to walk alone at night a mere two blocks from the main gate. Same thing with Portsmouth Shipyard, Pearl Harbor, and New London Submarine Base. In fact, in the case of New London, the Navy originally rejected the land and tried to close the base, only to be told by the sitting Representative of Connecticut, Edwin Higgins, to basically pack sand and stay there. The best way to describe the area around a base is with a movie quote from Star Wars where Obi-Wan Kenobi describes Mos Eisley as a "wretched hive of scum and villainy."

My family avoided the vape stores, pawn shops, and predatory lending car dealerships offering eighteen percent interest to all military buyers, but at some point, we had to eat. We decided to check out the nearby sushi restaurant, which offered all you can eat sushi at a great price. Since I have children that eat like adults, all you can eat is normally a great deal for my family. We all had smiles walking into the restaurant, and those smiles faded after five seconds upon entry. The restaurant was dark. We were the only people there. The waitress looked uninterested in being there. The sushi was not anything to write home about. We left and considered ourselves lucky to not be sick the next day.

Luckily, we didn't inhabit scum and villainy for long. Two days later we drove to The Amber, checked in and received the keys for our new apartment. Huzzah, I thought! We had already called two friends of ours, Gordon and Jason, to help us unload the storage unit with their trucks. We headed together to the storage unit and unloaded it all in one trip. Once we successfully lugged everything upstairs, we stared at our apartment, and the sheer emptiness of it hit me. It was pretty bare. We had a card table and some chairs in the living/dining room open concept combo space. And...that was about it. Seriously. Pretty empty. There was little excitement about the thought of surviving with three kids for three months in this place.

At that moment, Gordon ripped open his shirt to reveal a giant red "S" and announced that he was the real Superman! Well, OK, that didn't really happen. But he did tell us that he had an old couch he was throwing away this week, plus a folding table and some other chairs. That made him as good, if not better, than Superman for me at that moment. Gordon, Jason and I loaded into his truck and headed to his house. Gordon's couch wasn't in great condition, but it was clean and had cushions, and that was good enough for me. Plus, I heard that choosy beggars sit on the floor and eat off a scavenged tray table, and if I made my pregnant wife sit on the floor for three months, I might not live to see the birth of my child.

That evening I walked across the street and brought back pizza. The convenience of being able to walk to restaurants was new to me, since I had mostly lived in suburbia for the last fourteen years. My extremely hungry kids and wife made short work of the pizza, breadsticks and salad, and it wasn't long before the kids were in bed. I managed to setup our TV for antenna service so Rachel and I could watch local WAVY-10 news, and after a while I decided to step out onto our porch to enjoy the fresh air.

The air wasn't exactly fresh. As I stood on our porch on the second story of the three-story building, I noticed a small crowd. There were three young men in orbit around a young lady, and the whole group was smoking cigarettes. I say they orbited her on purpose, because while the three of them were in OK physical shape, the lady was not. She might have been the same weight as all three men combined. To me, it was obvious that the poor males were all trapped in this fat lady's gravitational well, unable to achieve escape velocity without additional assistance. Given that I noticed devices nearby that allowed for the smoking of non-tobacco products, I suspected that their fates were sealed, and at some point, gravity would cause a collision of bodies in the near future.

I walked back inside, and by 10:30 p.m. I was in bed. The ruckus from the orbiting masses outside our porch was getting louder, but I suspected that it might dissipate with a cloud of non-tobacco products, and it wasn't worth making our new neighbors angry on our first night. At three in the morning, I awoke to screaming and shouting. I lay in my bed while I listened to two of the males, apparently freed from orbit, screaming obscenities at each other. I could hear every word through our relatively thin walls. Most of those words were only four letters long, so I was doubtful that these people played a lot of Boggle or Scrabble in their free time. If I could hear what they were saying, so could my kids, so I called the security firm, which promised to send someone out right away.

The words got more heated, and more low-scoring four-lettered Scrabble phrases appeared. I distinctly remembered when, around 3:30 a.m., one of the Scrabble participants scored big with a fourteen-letter phrase, starting with the letter "F", that meant to end the other person's life. That got my attention, and my first thought was "If you're going to shoot him, please make it quick so I can get back to sleep." I must have mumbled those inside thoughts in my outside voice, because Rachel immediately replied "We don't need a dead body outside the apartment."

That point was very true. Plus, I'd feel somewhat obligated to lend medical assistance, and then the outside of the building would be a crime scene, which would make the drive to and from work difficult. I seriously didn't need any of those complications in my life, so I called 911. I told the operator that two men were threatening to shoot each other, that I was pretty scared and that this had been going on for the last hour. After I hung up the phone, I opened my small pistol safe, checked that my weapon was loaded, and put it back in the safe. I had defense in case the conflict spilled into my apartment, but I'm not the sheriff or law enforcement, and I had no intention of solving other people's problems that day.

Ten minutes passed, then a police vehicle rolled through the area. The Scrabble participants must have suspected something, because they had ended their low-scoring game by then. I drifted back off to sleep, pondering an eight-letter phrase for "made a poor choice when picking apartments."

Chapter 28
July 2018

If you've ever seen two dogs fight at a dog park, or two kids fight on a playground, you understand how difficult it is to break them apart and figure out who was responsible for what. When Otto the home designer wrote me back, I had that same feeling. Otto and Manius were essentially pointing fingers at each other because the city had not approved the house plans, and the problem was with trusses. Otto had written the plans to use trusses, because most homes use trusses and the city is used to seeing them. Manius was more familiar with stick framing roofs because that's what he used during renovations.

First, let's be completely honest here: trusses and stick framing are almost the same thing. Stick framing a roof means you take lumber and assemble it on site into the roof shape. Trusses are engineered, meaning someone else assembled them at a factory into a roof shape, then shipped them to your house to be placed onto your roof. Neither method is wrong, and Manius had asked Otto to make changes to the plans to reflect stick framing so he could resubmit it to the City of Chesapeake. Each time the City of Chesapeake found something wrong, it sent the plans back and Manius had to ask Otto to change it again. After multiple revisions, the City of Chesapeake suddenly declared that they needed a full site plan before approving the home, which would have required additional survey work at additional expense. Manius felt it was Otto's problem for not getting changes fixed sooner, and Otto blamed Manius for not getting it right the first time.

Who was at fault? I have no idea, even to this day. The first thing that struck me was that we didn't have an approved house plan from the city. What should have happened was that the house design, made by Otto, gets submitted along with other documents to the City government a long time before. The City approves the plan, which includes everything from sewer and water hookup fees to temporary power and school district issues. Once the City has approved the plan, the builder has a surveyor place four flags at the four corners of the foundation, and the foundation crew comes in and pours a concrete foundation.

No approved plan meant we were at square zero in the month I was supposed to originally move in. What I think happened was that Manius assumed everything would be straightforward with the City and the house plans, and didn't submit anything until the new year. By April, when the plan wasn't approved, he realized he was in trouble and started blaming everyone, from the City and Otto to the weather for the delay. Fun fact, City governments have a tendency to be slothful giant bureaucracies that move at whatever speed they want. In fact, for anyone that loves to rail against the U.S. federal government on social media, you really should pay more attention to what your local city government does, because they are significantly more important in your day-to-day life than any President or federal agency.

There wasn't much I could do, because the City and Manius had to work out their differences. I felt bad because initially I had taken a hard line with Otto, thinking that he was the problem. As more information emerged, it dawned on me I was probably wrong, so I called him to apologize for not having the whole picture. Large home builders have a whole department of people that just work plans through City governments, so this is never an issue when you buy a home from them. Manius didn't have that, so he was doing all these functions. I did sympathize, but the fact that this had gone on for so long without me knowing made me extremely wary. Like a dog that shies away from a hand after getting hit by someone, I was significantly less trusting at this point of what Manius told me.

While we navigated City government approval, Manius did receive permission to clear trees. I met him at the property one afternoon to select trees for clearing. In what would become the front yard there were multiple tall pine trees, some probably forty to fifty feet tall. I had Manius mark all of them, because I have a huge aversion to pine trees.

Pine trees are the melba toast of the tree world. Sure, if you're buying lumber, pine trees and fir trees make up the majority of lumber products, so they are useful in that regard. But for homeowners, pine trees are worthless, because they give you nothing. Pine needles are a fire hazard when dry. Pine cones become projectiles when you run them over with a lawnmower. Nothing dropped from a pine tree can be eaten. I don't even think they look all that pretty either. When I lived in Georgia, we had a nasty ice storm that rolled through and essentially coated the area in a sheet of ice. I walked on my back porch to see even the pine trees coated in a quarter inch or more of ice. To my horror, I watched as a tree suddenly snapped with a loud crack and sheared off. Thirty feet of tree collapsed onto the ground with no warning. Over the next week, as the area slowly thawed, I would hear snaps and cracks, and when it was safe to drive on the roads again, our area was littered with the remains of broken pine trees snapped off like tooth picks.

During the heat of the summer, with LuMa Construction raging against the machine that is City Hall, pine trees began to fall on my property. Finally, near the end of July, the city backed down from requiring LuMa Construction produce a full site plan, although they did nearly fine them for forgetting to put in a silt fence, which was a rule that the city only recently started enforcing. By now, Rachel was having more pregnancy-related nausea, and spent a lot of time resting on our air mattress of a bed. Receiving word that we had an approved plan and could finally start digging a foundation was pretty uplifting.

Chapter 29
July 2018

I returned to my apartment from work near the end of July to find a letter from Union Mortgage in my mailbox. I thought it was odd, mainly because Union preferred to do most of its business online, and hadn't physically sent me anything up to this point. Throwing it on the stack with the rest of the mail, I dropped it off on the kitchen counter and took out the garbage to our compactor. The Amber had a large garbage compactor where residents emptied their garbage, which is a fantastic idea, until you realize the utter laziness of many residents. Every time I moseyed over to the compactor, I would find piles of garbage teeming with flies and filth because nobody pressed the compactor button.

Seriously, it's not hard people! You put in your garbage, shut the door, and press the button. You don't even have to wait around or hold the button, because the machine runs a whole compactor cycle with one button push. Compacting the garbage pushes it into a container and keeps the smell and the insects away. It takes two seconds, maybe three if you're a bit arthritic or slow. Every gloomy trip I made to the compactor chipped away at the little faith left I had in humanity.

That remaining faith was put to the test when I returned and opened my mail. Union Mortgage sent me a nice, one-page letter that read something like this:

Dear Ryan,

    Thanks for being a great Union Mortgage customer! We know you have an account with us, and you went through a lot of pain to prove that you are really you, that you intend to repay your mortgage, that you don't somehow think the VA will pay for your mortgage for you, and that you're willing to sign lots of other papers just because we put them in your electronic box. Congratulations to you ole' chap!

    Union Mortgage is going out of business. If you don't finish your house in the next month, you'll have to find someone else to finance it. Cheerio sucker!

OK, maybe the "cheerio" and "ole' chap" parts are made up, but the part about Union going out of business? Totally true. Union Mortgage was part of Union Bank, which merged with another bank, and the resulting super-bank decided they didn't want to be in the mortgage business anymore. They decided to close Union Mortgage, and if you happened to be in the middle of a project, well, hurry up and finish.

Staring at this letter made me pause and think. First, had we finished construction on time, or were close to it, I wouldn't be in this trouble at all. Second, I couldn't imagine a situation where a mortgage company executive just wakes up one day and says "OK, it's time to close this company,

let's make that happen before close of business."
These sorts of things take a few months to work
out, so how in the heck was I just now getting
notified? Wouldn't Vance, Tatiana and Aurelia
have known this was coming, and if so, been
calling me to figure this out? Why the heck was all
the bad luck falling on me in July?

After giving the awful news to Rachel lying
down...yes, I literally laid down next to her on the
air mattress and told her the news, I called Vance
and left a message on his cell phone. I was
confused and a bit hurt, but I tried to stay
professional on the phone. By this point, I felt like
everyone was fleecing me. I had done my research,
had filled out forms quickly, and had refrained
from making last minute home design changes. I
had paid my bills on time. I had started this
project with enough time to finish it. Everyone else
seemed inclined to screw me over. LuMa
Construction grossly mismanaged their time, and
now not only was I stuck in a crappy apartment
with a pregnant wife and no real furniture, but
now I apparently didn't even have a mortgage
company.

Vance called back in less than an hour. He
wasn't surprised by the letter. Apparently, Union
had an automated system that spit letters out
without due regard for process. He did confirm
that Union Mortgage was closing, but the
mortgage office was spinning off into a company
called Federal Savings Bank, and my loan would
be transferred there. The move wasn't going to
happen until September, and he was still working

out details on how everything would transfer, which was why he hadn't told me about it. I thanked him and hung up the phone, then sat on our couch and stared at the wall.

That whole trust thing I had? Gone by this point. I didn't have a single person in the whole process I trusted anymore. Nobody was being upfront about anything. When a project is going well, everyone eagerly answers your calls. When things start going south, suddenly everyone clams up. Just when I need more communication seemed to be when people communicated less.

That night was an especially long one. I sat outside on our little porch and stared into the night while my family slept. I was tired of everything. I felt wore down and stuck. I couldn't just up and drop out of the home building process, but it appeared that everyone was just screwing me over, and I could do nothing about it. Here I was, thinking I was building our dream home for my family, and instead we were stuck in a small apartment, having paid a bunch of money already for a piece of land that didn't have a house on it. I questioned myself a lot that night as I slowly sipped a scotch.

I also sat on the porch because it scared away fat lady and her orbiting male moons. They tended to hang out elsewhere when I was on the porch, and I was perfectly OK with that.

J uly was a busy month. I lost faith in LuMa Construction, the City of Chesapeake, Union Mortgage and the whole home building process. I still couldn't tell if I had a shred of faith in humanity, but my garbage compactor trips were doing a number on that too.

But, on the bright side, we broke ground on the house. Manius called me with great news: the city backed off from insisting on a full site plan and they were digging the foundation that day. About two days later, I stopped by to see the results.

Foundations are impressive. It's the concrete that holds up your house, taking all the weight from above it and dispersing it into the ground below in such a way that you don't sink into the mud. Manius walked me around the foundation, showing where the specified four corners were and verifying they were square for me. That was a nice touch. Every builder knows how to verify a corner is square, but it was nice to see it done in person.

We were nearing the end of July, and I wanted to give Rachel some hope. Her pregnancy was particularly rough, and the Virginia heat and humidity in the middle of July was too often unbearable for her. She spent a lot of time cooped up in the apartment resting on the air mattress. She had only seen the property once, when it was still heavily wooded, so seeing an actual shape that resembled our future house would be a boost for her morale.

One thing she had done recently was pick out the brick for our house. A few days after we moved into our apartment, we stopped by the brick and stone store that LuMa used and picked out a brick color and design for the crawl space and our fireplace. Having never picked out brick colors, I figured there was a grand total of five, maybe six brick types. Boy was I wrong! Rachel and I walked into the store with the walls jam packed with brick swatches, which are one-foot by one-foot pieces of carboard with a brick design on them. They had red bricks, and black bricks, and yellow-ish bricks, and bricks that looked like stone, and stone that had bricks on it, and more! It was a veritable brick nirvana.

The store employee greeted us and brought out several samples. They also knew our vinyl siding color, so they recommended bricks with complementary color tones. If the term "complementary color tones" seems weird to you, you're not alone. I'm not an artist, and while I can see color just fine, I'm not the best person to pick out "complementary color tones." That's what Rachel is for. She waded through brick designs with ease, parting the non-complementary color tones to one side like Moses parting the Red Sea with a simple gesture of his staff. It wasn't long before she had selected a red brick with some beige tones.

I always wondered what happens when colors clash. Do the primary colors fight to prevent being mixed up into secondary colors? Do all colors bleed red when damaged, or do they bleed their respective color? Do colors form alliances? I figure garish colors just sort of get along with everyone, since who the heck wants to fight a purple and green combination?

None of these questions in my head were answered at the masonry shop, but we did see engineered stone. For our wood fireplace, we wanted a stone veneer that made it "pop" when you walked in. "Pop" is another one of those fancy artistic terms that refers to catching the eye when you walk in a room. In this case it's not a reference to the carbonated beverages from the Coca Cola company, which are only called pop if you come from the Midwest. Otherwise, you might refer to such things as "soda," or worse, call every carbonated beverage a "coke!" The masonry store had several engineered stone patterns to see. Engineered stone simply means the stone was made in a plant using masonry fragments and dust that are pressed into molds. In the past, engineered stone looked bland and dull, but better technology has produced realistic stone that appears to have been mined out of the ground. They all have cool names, such as "Charleston Ledge" and "Mountain Top," and they vary in how many different stone types make up each pattern. Engineered stone also has a full range of colors, since, you know, you wouldn't want colors clashing. Think about the savage battles between the colors in your fireplace and the colors in the wall. You might have to repaint the walls to cover up all the color blood left behind from the losing side. Luckily these thoughts did not escape from my head, lest the masonry people think I was crazy. We finished picking out our stone designs and left the store, and I saw a smile sneak onto Rachel's face.

It was raining at the end of July when we drove out to our house. Manius had the foundation guys adding the brick on the outside of the crawl space. I recognized the brick at once and pointed it out to Rachel, the smile creeping back into her weary face. We walked up and Manius introduced us to Rick, the brick supervisor. Rick was in ankle high water and knee-deep Virginia clay, and seemed to be having the time of his life. Covered in sticky clay, we bumped fists instead of shaking hands, and he described the progress he had made today despite the rain.

The muddy site reminded me of just how vulnerable we were to weather. Even in 2018, the weather still dictated much of what we could do. Rain and heat, snow and ice, and everything in between could bring work on a job site to a crashing halt. Manius was desperate to arrive at the point where the house was framed and had a roof. Once the roof was on, multiple specialties, such as plumbing, electrical and cabinets, could happen at once. Until that point, everything had to happen in a specific order, and that order was too often subject to the weather.

I thanked Manius and Rick and we headed home. Rachel was tired, but she was smiling, because she could imagine the house going up on the foundation. It was finally becoming a reality that we could see and touch, even if encased in clay soil and threatening to be drowned out by the rain.

July had been a hard month, but as it came to an end, we were finally tracking to resolve all the big headaches and problems that would hold us up. With those out of the way, it was time to watch the magic of our forever home being built.

Chapter 31
August 2018

August in southeast Virginia is hot. It's also muggy since there is plenty of water nearby, from both the Great Dismal Swamp and the Atlantic Ocean. This dials up the humidity level so high that you often feel that you are drinking the air around you. It is a nasty time to do any work outside, and it is exactly when our house was framed.

Framing involves a couple of steps. First, the builder attaches boards of pressure treated wood to the concrete foundation. This is called a sill plate. Everything else is built off this sill plate, and if termites attack your house, it's likely the first place they would be found since the plate is close to the ground. In times past, builders would "shoot in" bolts by pushing them into the dried concrete with a driver that uses a 22-caliber bullet (just the gunpowder with no bullet). For our house, Lucius sunk in long bolts, called J-bolts, into the wet concrete so that the threaded portion sat above the concrete. He then drilled holes in the sill plate boards and put them over the J-bolts. Then it was a quick matter of threading on a nut, and the sill plate was attached quite securely to the home's foundation.

On top of the sill plate sits the subfloor. In our case, it's a 2x6 piece of wood that is placed upright so that there is a six-inch gap above the sill plate. Other 2x6s are placed on the sill plate and laid out in a pattern to create the frame that will hold up your floor. On top of that is plywood or OSB (Oriented Strand Board), which is what your flooring sits on. The first-floor walls also attach to this board.

At the end of August, I stopped by with my son in the evening to check out how the framing was progressing. We drove up to the site and the first-floor walls were pretty much all installed. I decided to spot check a few things, the first being the labels on the sill plates. Every piece of pressure treated wood gets a little label describing the pressure treatment type and grade. Thankfully, all of my home's wood came from a company in North Carolina, was treated with micronized copper azole, and was rated for ground contact.

My next step was checking the studs. If you've ever purchased 2x4s from Home Depot, you appreciate the fact that wood is all too often not particularly straight. I walked through every, single room and looked at every, single 2x4. No joke. And there are a lot of 2x4s on just the first level of the house! To my pleasant surprise, all of them were straight and properly attached. There wasn't a defective 2x4 on the entire first floor of the house.

We did find one problem though. I walked to where the guest bathroom was, and didn't see a window. Next to the bathroom is a closet, which had a window in exactly the same shape as the missing bathroom window. "Hmm" I thought. I took a picture and sent it to Manius. He texted back with "Yup, that's definitely wrong, we'll move it." Since we caught it early, it's really easy to move a window during the framing portion of a home's construction. It only took maybe an hour the next day and the window was in the correct spot.

Framing is amazing in that it goes up quite fast. I took pictures of the first-floor framing on August 25, and when I came back on September 2, the second floor was framed, and sheathing was on about seventy-five percent of the house. Sheathing is the OSB or plywood that sits on the outside of an exterior wall. If you cut a slice of a home wall and looked at it from the side, it would sort of resemble a cake. Not a cake you would eat unless you're a termite or a masochist, but a cake in that it has different layers inside it, each for different reasons. The outermost layer is your siding, normally vinyl or brick. Below that is a plastic wrap, and after that is sheathing, the OSB or plywood that provides a place to attach the siding. Then comes the wall, a 2x4 or 2x6 framed box where your electrical, plumbing, and other things are routed. Exterior walls are typically filled with insulation, either the pink stuff that comes in a roll or spray foam. This insulation keeps the outside air and moisture away from the inside and keeps your nice conditioned air inside. The part on the inside you see is painted drywall that is nailed or screwed to the wall itself.

The sheathing on our house used the Zip system. Normally builders put up OSB and then cover it with a plastic material, referred to as house wrap, to make it waterproof. The problem with this is that if you don't seal all the right spots there are opportunities for moisture to leak into the walls. Water is the absolute worst enemy to a house. It'll warp and mold wood, wear away at concrete over time, and even attempt to break down brick. Instead of house wrap, the Zip system actually comes in prebuilt pieces with a waterproof layer on one side bonded to the OSB at a factory. That bonding prevents any chance of water intrusion, and so long as you seal the joints between pieces with Zip tape, your house is perfectly waterproof, and even comes with a warranty.

Walking through the upstairs, I was again pleasantly surprised to find no framing issues. LuMa Construction might suck at timelines, but at least when they build something, they build it right. Next door to us is a residential neighborhood being built by a well-known large building company. I decided to walk through one of the homes that was also framed but not yet sheathed. Sadly, there were a lot of cheap wall studs, the 2x4s that go straight up and down in a wall. You'll never see it on a finished product because the wall will be covered in drywall, but the poor workmanship was really obvious to me, especially compared to LuMa Construction's work.

Chapter 32
September 2018

September brought another letter from Union Mortgage, announcing that it had morphed into Federal Savings Bank, once again confirming that bank employees charged with creating brand names lack all forms of imagination. September also brought sheathing and roofing. After Labor Day weekend, my house actually resembled a house, just missing the inside walls, doors, windows, heating and cooling, and all the other niceties a real house has. But hey, at least the roof was on!

September is prime hurricane season for Hampton Roads. Hurricanes generally don't make landfall in Hampton Roads, but it does happen, and when it does, we receive tons of rain and lots of wind. I had specifically talked with Manius about the best way to keep a roof from getting damaged by hurricanes. Originally, I had wanted a metal roof, but the additional thirty-five thousand dollars was not in the budget, as I just don't have that sort of money sitting around. Surprisingly, Manius was fine with an asphalt roof. He told me the most important thing was the number of nails per shingle. Most roofs in the area have high quality shingles that can survive storm damage, but installers go cheap on nails and only uses two per shingle. If you install four per shingle, the shingles are more resistant to high winds, and you preserve the manufacturer's thirty-year warranty.

Stupid things like this always made me ponder why people are so cheap. I didn't want to guess how many nails were in the shingles of our nearby neighbor's homes being constructed by a large construction company.

Now that my home resembled a real home, I wanted to have a family visit to help raise our spirits. We had just started school, and we were allowed to attend the school our home was districted for, but Rachel had to drive the kids to school and back every, single day. It wasn't a short drive either. Had I thought this through, I would have picked an apartment closer to our school. Then again, I also looked for places with three-month leases, and if you're paying attention to your home building disaster bingo card, you realize that I rolled over three months in September. Yup. Thus, I had to extend our lease, at a particularly expensive month-to-month rate. Between the expensive lease and long drives to and from school, we needed something positive.

We drove up to the home and the kids gleefully explored the house, marking off their bedrooms and already negotiating for more space. Rachel and I walked a bit slower through the house, making sure that rooms were correctly laid out. The framing for our peninsula style fireplace was in, which was really cool to see. I could finally imagine where our furniture would be placed. Discussing where our couch would be cheered Rachel up. Visiting the home was a resounding success.

As we drove back to our apartment, we realized that it would be time to purchase appliances. We hadn't done that yet because there had been no need. Appliances typically improve over time, so purchasing early doesn't benefit you. It does take a while to ship appliances in, so we couldn't wait too long. Manius agreed to store the appliances at his shop, so I pulled out my appliance research to make one last update.

Appliances are expensive. We were purchasing a stove, refrigerator, dishwasher and range hood. At our previous house in Connecticut, we had been forced to use an off-brand electric stove. It took forever to heat up the oven, and I seriously mean forever. I would turn the oven to 350 degrees Fahrenheit and wait for nearly an hour for it to heat up to temperature. I remember waking up early on Thanksgiving just to start the stove, like I was living in colonial times. I had used wood stoves in the past that warmed up faster. I once had to call Rachel from the grocery store to tell her I was heading home and to go ahead and start the oven so we could eat dinner on time. After dealing with that, I never again wanted a pathetic, underpowered oven.

Sadly, in that same house, the dishwasher was nearly as pathetic. It really wasn't much of a dish washer per say, more resembling a "throw soapy water at our dishes in a random pattern" device. I could probably have put our dishes out in the rain and they would have been cleaned better. Our dishes always came out not very clean, not very rinsed, and kind of gross. We almost always had to wash them again and rinse them off in the sink, and for any small loads, I was more inclined to hand wash, since it was faster.

So naturally, we were especially inclined to purchase high quality appliances. For our stove, we purchased a double oven with an induction cooktop. Induction is this old technology that is making a comeback. The stove top is a large electromagnet that induces (hence the name) a current in any ferrous metal pan set on top of it. Induction cooktops have been around forever, but fell out of style when people began using more aluminum cooking pans, which aren't magnetic. Now that manufacturers can layer iron in the bottom of a pan and then coat it with aluminum, most pots and pans are capable of induction cooking.

I really wanted an induction cooktop for two reasons. First, they are extremely efficient. They use less electricity than a standard cooktop, and they heat faster than a gas cooktop. My friends in love with their gas cooktops often debate me on that point, but I did a side-by-side comparison, and the induction boils water faster than gas, hands down. This saves me from paying extra for a gas line in the house. My other reason for using induction is safety. The cooking surface doesn't heat up. Well, ok, to be technically correct, it gets warm because the pan transfers some of the heat onto the stove. But it is significantly less hot than an electric burner, and if a small child puts their hands on it, they won't burn their hands. Since I have children, and a baby coming on the way, this point was extremely important.

Now, the double oven part is tricky. Why a double oven? Well, one reason is parties. When we have people come over for a meal, or family stay with us, we have to cook a lot of food. In the past, we could only have one oven at one temperature, and if you cooked a large turkey, essentially you couldn't cook anything else. A double oven opens the door to many more options. You can cook two dishes at two different temperatures. Or, if you're grilling, you can set one oven to "keep warm" your burgers while the other cooks your side dishes. The possibilities are endless, and it makes hosting friends and family much less stressful.

The only problem is that there was exactly one induction double oven, a beautiful, expensive Kitchen Aide. As much as I didn't want to, I bit the bullet and purchased that model. That used up fifty percent of our appliance budget, not leaving much space for our refrigerator, range hood and dishwasher. Luckily, we found a cheaper refrigerator that did not have an in-door water dispenser. This worked for us because that is the most likely item to break on a refrigerator, so we would save ourselves on repair costs in the long run. We also found a very nice Kenmore dishwasher and a range hood on sale. I ordered all the appliances from the local Navy Exchange and set them up for delivery to Manius' shop. The store employee said it would take nearly a month, so I was a bit worried that we would move in before

Halloween and have no appliances. Thinking about that now, I chuckle to myself.

Chapter 33
October 2018

September came and passed, and October arrived with little fanfare. I fell into the routine of working out at the nearby YMCA in the morning, going to work, coming home, reviewing house progress and keeping a watchful eye outside of our apartment for smoking parties that would spiral into early morning screaming matches. Rachel drove kids back and forth, growing more tired as the new baby grew in size. Our house slowly creeped along, and soon Manius' promise of "done before Halloween" morphed into "done before Thanksgiving."

At this point, I didn't trust Manius or Lucius about anything concerning timelines. Their idea of when something would be finished was entirely off mark. It was obvious that they had started too late and were playing catch up. I couldn't really fire them though. It was going to be a slog to finish the house, but we had to do it together. Every time I would drive by the house after work, I would see the nearby homes being completed faster than mine. They had siding, electrical, plumbing, a roof, and in October, started having people move in. Meanwhile, my house sat nearby, sad and unfinished, while my family languished in a crappy apartment. Life felt pretty unfair.

I was also getting worried about clothing. We were approaching winter, and we didn't have any winter clothing. All of our stuff was in storage, and since we had moved in June, we had put all the cold weather clothes in our household good shipment. Now that it was October, the air was changing. It was still hot, being Virginia and all, but fall was upon us. It wouldn't be long before Crocs and shorts weren't viable fashion options. We could buy more clothes, but anyone that has purchased kids clothing before understands the high costs involved, especially since the Goodwill in Virginia didn't always have the correct sizes for our kids.

Luckily, social media saved me. I posted on Facebook about our situation, and my phone lit up. Our friends in Virginia scoured their closets and found cold weather kid and maternity clothing. A fellow cryptologist living in Maryland sent us a huge box of her kid's old winter gear. After lugging it up our stairs, I opened it and experienced an early Christmas. Boots, shoes, socks, coats, hats...you name it, she had packed it. I'm guessing it was easily five hundred dollars in clothing. Given that we were stretched thin, paying a mortgage and rent, plus using more gas than normal to drive everywhere, it seriously saved us from hardship.

October did bring wiring and plumbing. The electrician came in and began stringing wiring in the studs. I have an uncle that is an electrician, so I would send the occasional photo to him, and his responses were encouraging: everything looked proper and was very much up to code. I was surprised at just how fast he could string wire. In less than a week the house had outlet boxes in every room, with wires running down to the breaker box.

Our plumber was an interesting fellow. Rachel and I brought the family to visit the house, and we saw the truck with the name "Plumber Bob" on the outside. When we walked in, a very large man in a set of overalls greeted us. His overalls had a nametag with the name "Stan" on it, so I assumed his name was Stan.

"Nice to meet you Stan!" I said, and was surprised to receive a weird look on his face.

"I'm Bob" he replied

"Uhm, my bad, but you've got a nametag that says Stan"

Bob looked down and mumbled, quite matter-of-factly, "Oh, never mind that."

Bob, as I now knew him, was best described as a good-ole' boy from the country. He spoke with such a drawl that often times I struggled to understand exactly what he was saying. It felt like being in Scotland. I had traveled there before and while I could understand the women when they spoke, many of the men spoke in such a low tone and heavy accent that I couldn't understand them. I mean, I could tell they were speaking English, but the English words were traversing a fog that distorted them beyond recognition. Bob's language was similar. He was obviously speaking English, but there were inside jokes and references I just couldn't pick up on.

While Bob wasn't an orator, he was a seriously talented plumber. We walked through every room, and he pointed out how water came in and how it left through the drains. I paid attention to the piping and smiled at the sight of nail guards in all the right spots. Plumbing in a wall should have metal where there is a chance someone would bang a nail into it. It's not uncommon for cheap plumbing to skip this step, but Bob had installed it correctly.

Bob said he had a question about the plumbing in our master bathroom. Bob, Manius, Rachel and I walked up to our master bedroom, which had the tub sitting in the center of the room, still wrapped in protective cellophane. I smiled looking at it. The tub that I had spent so much time picking out was finally here. It looked great, and I knew I could actually fit in it once it was installed.

Bob broke my smile by pointing out that my wonderful tub was six inches too long to fit into its space. He suggested moving a wall, which brought a frown from Manius. We COULD move a wall, but it would require a deviation from plan, which would require a city inspector to sign off on the change. Given the attention the house already had from the city, it was best to not move walls.

Rachel asked "What if we make the shower smaller?" The shower was next to the tub, but it was a tile shower and hadn't been finished yet. Manius liked that idea, but I had an issue with it. "The shower head comes out from the wall, so it'll be a little tight on space. Can we install a waterfall shower head instead?"

Problem solved. I hadn't wanted a waterfall shower head coming from the ceiling, but if we left the shower head in the wall, it wouldn't leave much useable space in the shower. A waterfall shower head made the whole shower useable, and in hindsight was something we should have requested in the first place. Bob was pleased, since moving the shower head was pretty straightforward and even made the tiling job for the shower easier. We planned to return in a few days to see how everything panned out.

Chapter 34
October 2018

A few days passed, and I was itching to see the house again. Now that it had plumbing and electrical, it was easy to imagine situating our furniture. That provided excitement, a bump to our mood that was gloomy from missing the first moving date of what would be many empty promises from LuMa Construction.

I also wanted to take some video of the walls before they were closed up with drywall. Anyone that has renovated a home knows that when you open up a wall, you typically don't know what you'll encounter on the inside. My dad had suggested taking a video of all the walls to show how the electrical and plumbing lines traversed them. This would help if I ever wanted to add an outlet or drill into a wall, because I would have a good idea of what lay on the other side of the drywall. That would allow better planning for any future renovation.

On a slightly windy day in October, I loaded up the family and headed to the house. The day was a bit cooler, but on the way over it started to rain. No big deal, since the house had a roof, we could still visit. As we neared our destination, the rain was getting worse. I decided it would be good to pull right up to the garage so we could minimize just how wet we would get on the short jaunt from the car to the house. Our Toyota Highlander made it just fine, and soon we were exploring our home.

I took a particularly long and detailed video of all the downstairs walls. I had to speak really loudly to be heard over the pounding sound of the rainstorm. Man, it was raining really, really hard! After I had meticulously documented the downstairs floor, I walked upstairs where the roaring rainstorm noise was even more oppressive. I took another long, boring video of all the walls to capture the details I would need later in life.

Rachel and I also saw the final product for our master bathroom. Now the tub fit into the space without any issues. The shower, despite being cut down, felt really big. We both stepped into the space and there was plenty of room to move around. The kids were downstairs, and we both pondered, albeit briefly, how well the rainstorm masked any noises coming from the bathroom and how it appeared that you could make an awful lot of noise without anyone hearing anything downstairs...if you know what I mean.

Video and exploring completed, we decided it was time to depart. The family loaded into the car, and I started navigating the murky driveway that seemed to have disappeared during the rainstorm. As we pulled out, I felt the car starting to sink. Thinking quickly, I put the car in Low Gear and tried to push through mud.

My efforts met with utter, complete failure. Two of our four tires sunk into the mud and spun freely without grip. I put the vehicle in reverse to rock us out, but that effort failed as well. We were now hopelessly stuck in the mud. Rachel called USAA, and the very pleasant person on the line informed us that it would be about three hours before we could get towed out.

I have to pause here and complain about roadside assistance. The concept of paying for roadside assistance heavily relies on getting somewhat timely roadside assistance. But every, single time I have called to get roadside assistance, it takes them hours to get to me. Every time. I've clocked and logged these events, so I'm not fabricating these frustrations. Half the time, I end up bailing myself out, and the other half of the time, a friend reaches us and helps us. Roadside assistance, you are dead to me as a concept!

A nearby friend came to our rescue. Jason, who had earlier watched Gordon rip open his shirt to reveal he was Superman (not really, but I'm using that joke for all its worth), now had the chance to challenge Gordon with his own super accomplishments. I called Jason to let him know I was stuck, and he immediately headed to the nearby store to purchase a ratcheting come-along. This fancy device lets you connect one vehicle to another at the towing points. You then ratchet the straps tight and then slowly drive both vehicles in the same direction. Ideally, the pulling force of the non-stuck vehicle is enough to yank the stuck vehicle out until traction is restored.

Ideally. Our Toyota Highlander is a pretty heavy vehicle, and Jason's vehicle isn't any bigger. This attempt could also get both vehicles stuck. Complicating that, it was still raining, and now the kids were complaining about needing to use the bathroom. Rachel and I were, not surprisingly, a bit stressed.

Jason arrived and he and I hooked up the vehicles. We tightened down the come-along and then I had him slowly pull forward until there was no slack in the strap. I made sure my family stayed safely inside the house, protected in case the strap snapped under tension. I then called Jason from my cell phone, and on the same count, we both moved our vehicles.

It was a resounding "blah" of a moment. Nothing happened. Jason's vehicle just wasn't big enough.

Refusing to give up, I had Jason take the tension out and I attached the come-along on a different tow point. This time, the force of Jason's vehicle would pull the front slightly to the left. My hope was this would drag the driver side tire into more stable ground, where it might pick up traction. Jason and I, now thoroughly soaked from the continuing rainstorm, tried again.

This time, success! The Highlander lurched from the mud, slinging a large wad of clay into the woods in its last act of defiance before the come-along redirected it to the driveway. Quickly we stopped, detached the come-along, loaded the family in and off we drove. A brief stop at the nearby 7-11 served to relieve our growing biological issues, and then off we trekked, wet and a bit muddy, to our apartment.

I called Jason later to thank him and ask for one more favor. Halloween was only a few days away, and the kids wanted to go trick or treating, but the apartment wasn't a great place for that, for obvious reasons. Jason and his wife Holli solved our problem by inviting us to visit their neighborhood instead. I decided to Google search Halloween in our local area and was surprised to learn that it was technically illegal for thirteen-year-olds and older to go trick-or-treating. Apparently, way back in the past some teenagers had used Halloween as an excuse to cause mischief (surprise!), so the city had passed an ordinance to ban it. Which, considering that many teenagers would take their younger siblings door to door for Halloween, seemed really dumb. The city hadn't enforced the ordinance, but it became the talk of the news in the days leading up to Halloween. Luckily for us, we enjoyed a teenager and mischief free Halloween with our friends that year.

Chapter 35
November 2018

As the leaves began turning different colors in Hampton Roads, I became increasingly red with anger. At the beginning of the month, Manius, once again, said he didn't think they could finish before Thanksgiving. Now we were approaching six months overdue. Had he told me the truth the first time, I could have gotten a better apartment in a nicer area at a cheaper rate. Now, I was getting really worried about our finances. We were paying higher than normal rent, plus we were making an interest-only mortgage payment on a house that wasn't quite complete, but close enough that the payment was getting large. My bank account was definitely feeling the squeeze.

I think I should take a minute here to again point out how important it is to sock away a lot of money before building a house. I had made pretty good money when we were assigned to Hawaii, and because I had shopped at the on-base commissary and spent more time at the beach than expensive restaurants, I had a lot of cash saved up. Most people understand that there are closing costs in a mortgage and a down payment if you can make one. When you build a house, there are a lot more hidden costs that nobody seems to talk about.

Start with land prep. Unless your lot is flat grass, you pay to clear trees. Even if its flat, you pay to bring in sand and gravel to build a pad to put your house on. You need a pad so that the water drains away from the house. In our case, the builder cleared about half an acre of heavy woods, to the tune of 10,000 dollars.

Then there are surveys. You can't use an existing survey, you need a new one, so you pay a company about five hundred dollars to survey your land. Make sure they draw where your house will be on the survey, or you'll pay them another couple hundred dollars to come back and draw a few lines that say "house" on that survey. Otherwise, the city will be displeased and won't approve your house plan.

Some fees are completely under your control, such as change fees. If you keep changing what you want, your builder has to take significant changes to the city for approval. Move a wall, add a garage or take out a window, and the whole set of plans needs a city engineer to stamp approve. It might take a day. Actually, no, it's the city government with a hulking bureaucracy, so we're talking a week, and potentially a 'stop work' situation depending on where you are in the process.

Then tack on the continuing interest-only mortgage payment, and all that hard earned, saved up money you thought you had suddenly vanishes into thin air.

So, when Manius promised that we'd move in by Christmas, I just rolled my eyes. My civility was finally slipping a bit. Manius in person was a really nice guy, and I try to be really forgiving when people fall short. Stuff happens, I get it. But my finances were getting burned at an astounding rate. I was seriously worried about dipping too deeply into our reserves. What happens if a big, nasty expense hits us suddenly? We had been lucky in that besides the house, nothing else bad had happened to our family. Our cars were fine, my job was secure, and I didn't make any poor investment decisions. But if something else happened, I might not be able to pay for any more surprises.

Amidst this gloom and doom, there was a bit of hot news. Our wood burning fireplace arrived and was installed in the living room. There was an initial snafu when Manius placed the order. He called Rachel and said "So I'm ordering your gas fireplace...", and Rachel instantly interrupted with "What gas fireplace?" Apparently, the plans had listed a gas fireplace by mistake. A quick fix and sign off by the city let us continue with a wood fireplace.

Another fireplace snafu happened when the fireplace arrived. The flooring around a wood fireplace must be fireproof and extend out a foot from any area a spark can fly out, plus it must extend back another foot. The "back another foot" part was a problem, because it backed up into our bar area and prevented the cabinets from opening. The solution meant bringing the fireplace out further into the room. There was a limit to how far you could move it because the exhaust piping can only make so many bends, otherwise the smoke won't exhaust correctly. Thankfully, the piping could make the angle without closing off the room.

The engineered stone for the fireplace had also arrived. It sat on the floor like a disassembled LEGO set. The person Manius had picked for the job spread the pieces out over nearly half of the living room. Painstakingly, he selected each piece to cover up the area above and below the fireplace. Piece by piece, he built our fireplace exterior. It took days for him to complete, and it was really cool to watch the pattern slowly emerge on the wall and floor. After a solid week of tiling, we stopped by to see the final result, and it was stunning. Seriously stunning.

The same tiling person was also selected to tile our master shower. He asked me what sort of design I wanted. I hadn't thought that much about the shower design. I decided on a light/dark sequence, with lighter colored tiles on the top and darker colored tiles on the bottom, which appear natural since shadows fall on the ground. To separate the dark and light tiles I imagined turning the square tiles on a point so that there was a diamond shape in between the two colors. Since describing what was in my head is difficult, I sketched all this on a scrap sheet of paper with a nearby pencil.

Three days later, I stopped by again to check on progress. I sucked my breath in when I walked into the master bathroom because the tiling job was amazing. Simply amazing. I had to hand it to our tiling guy, while he might have taken some time, he absolutely crushed it when he finished a job.

That bit of wondrous news helped buffer the fact that we spent Thanksgiving in an apartment. We invited one of our single friends that lived in the area over for Thanksgiving dinner, as I insisted that we maintain some semblance of normalcy despite our living conditions. Luckily our oven didn't take thirty minutes to heat up, so we could bake a turkey and a number of other meals without too much effort. We didn't have much in terms of seating though, as plastic chairs and a folding table was the best we could do. While Thanksgiving 2018 wasn't as glorious as previous years, we still managed to share it with good friends, cook good food and hold loud, raucous discussions with some much-needed laughter.

Thanksgiving was barely over when Manius called me out of the blue. The first words out of his mouth were "Hey Ryan, we've got a problem." That gave me the burning desire to respond with "Hey Captain Obvious, maybe you didn't notice you're six months behind schedule…", but I restrained myself. "OK, what problem do we have now?" I asked.

"The city won't let us hook up to sewer."

"What?!?" was the best I could blurt out.

Manius had just received a call from the city engineering department, which told him he couldn't hook up the house to city sewer. The city told him the house does not "have access to the city sewer line." "But that doesn't make sense, didn't we already pay the city for a sewer hookup?" I asked. "We did," replied Manius, "and I can see the sewer pumping station from your house, but the city won't budge." After processing that information, I asked "Well, what can we do?" Manius paused, then responded "Maybe dig a septic tank?"

No way, I thought. A basic septic system is at least 30,000 dollars, and because the Hampton Roads area has a high-water table, it's normally more expensive than that. I couldn't afford a septic system with my finances. And I certainly couldn't afford the time lost. It takes at least a month to receive the permit, dig, install and inspect a septic tank.

"Let me think of what to do" I told Manius, then hung up the phone. I just sat there stunned for a long while. I felt like the city government was cheating me out of a home. I had done everything correctly, and some loser bureaucrat at the city was screwing me. I just imagined some fat pig of a person sitting behind a desk, munching on potato chips and laughing as he stamped "Denied" on my sewer permit. "Maniacal laugh" the bureaucrat would say, and all of his fellow bureaucrats in neighboring cubicles would laugh out loud with him in unison. My dad had always warned me that local governments can be way worse than any state or federal government because they control things that matter to you on a daily basis. While my first thought was to fight, I then thought "Fight city hall?" The city could pull from limitless resources and drag out any court case, while I languished without a house and went broke.

A tear formed in the corner of my eye. Then another, and another, as I tried to wipe them away. This was it. My dreams were crushed. I had no recourse, no way to beat this. After all this work, after all this money sunk into what was supposed to be forever home, I had lost. Between LuMa Construction's total incompetence, the mortgage company going out of business, and now the city government screwing me over, I was in a corner that I couldn't recover from.

The part that really made me livid was that the house was down the street from Rebecca's eventual resting place. I was close to finishing all the arrangements to have her re-interred in a grave at a nearby cemetery. This would make it easy for my family to visit her on a regular basis. But that wouldn't work if I was broke. Red hot anger flashed in my blood. The city was essentially stomping on Rebecca's grave right in front of my face, without any chance of justice for me.

Now I understood why people like Marvin Heemeyer lost his mind. Marvin owned a muffler shop in Granby, Colorado. He got screwed over by the city government when they rezoned property next to him to build a concrete plant, blocking his access to his muffler shop. When he appealed, the city instead fined him for not hooking up to city sewer. The irony was that because the sewer line was over sixty feet away, the city wanted him to pay nearly 80,000 dollars to hook up. Marvin refused, and over the next year and a half he armored a Komatsu bulldozer with steel plates, cameras and gun ports. In June 2004 he went on a rampage, destroying the nearby concrete plant, city hall, the home of the former mayor, a judge's house, and a number of other buildings associated with people that had screwed him. When his bulldozer got stuck, he committed suicide instead of surrendering to the police.

I wasn't going to build a Killdozer, nor hurt anyone, but I certainly understood the white-hot anger of an oppressive city government killing my dreams. I texted my friend John, who worked in Navy construction, for advice.

Me: "John, you're a Seabee, what can I do?"

John: "Dude, you should Facebook the Mayor."

Me: "Really? That seems like a Millenial thing to do. I doubt he would even care."

John: "No man, he does. He'll reply back."

Since I had nothing better in mind, I found Mayor West's Facebook page and sent him the following message:

> *"Dear Mayor West, I'm trying to build a house in your city. My house is almost complete, but your city engineers are now saying I cannot hookup to city sewer, even though I paid the hookup fee a long time ago and my builder filed all the paperwork correctly. I can see the sewer station from the house, but your engineers won't help me. As a future city resident, I'm asking you to help me hook up to city sewer."*

I seriously did not expect the mayor to care or even respond. My phone rang the next day.

Me: "Hello this is Ryan"

Robert: "Hello Ryan, my name is Robert Geis, and I'm the Deputy City Manager for the City of

Chesapeake. I heard you're trying to hook up to city sewer, is that correct?"

Whoa, I thought. Facebook actually did something positive for a change.

Me: "Yes sir, I'm having some issues with that. I think we can find a way to hook up if your engineering team could work with my builder a bit."

Robert: "I took a look at where you're at, and I think we can manage that. You're in the Navy right?"

Me: "Yes sir, I work over at Second Fleet right now."

Robert: "Ahh, my buddy Woody is over there. Say hello to him next time you see him."

I thought really hard at this point. Who the heck was Woody? Ohhh....that was the Admiral's nickname. Double whoa, Mr. Geis knows my big boss. Luckily that works in my favor.

Me: "I'll absolutely let the Admiral know you said hello."

We talked a bit longer, and I focused on giving enough details about my background that Mr. Geis would be sympathetic to my situation. By the time I checked my email, I had a message from him directing his engineering team to "find a good solution" to this problem.

Manius called me an hour later. The "good solution" was a sewer lateral line connecting my house to the sewer line. The shocking part of said good solution was it cost **$18,536.75**. Even worse, Manius quoted the letter he had been emailed, which declared "A deposit in this amount is needed before the contractor can be authorized to begin the installation."

Funny enough, I did not have **$18,536.75** sitting around in a bank account collecting dust. We couldn't remove anything from the scope of the house because it was essentially near completion. I would need a loan, but I didn't have collateral for the loan. Desperate, I called Navy Federal Credit Union, where I had an account.

Me: "Hi, I need a loan for 18,000 dollars to be able to hook up my house to city sewer."

Navy Federal Employee: "Hmmm, we can't issue personal loans over 10,000 dollars."

Me: "OK, but do you have any other options?"

Navy Federal Employee: *rustling paper noises and soft whispers on the other end of the phone*

Me: "Uhmmm..."

Navy Federal Employee: "Hmm, it sounds like you're making a home improvement, riiight?"

Me: "Yessss..."

Navy Federal Employee: "Oh, well great news! You're approved for a home improvement loan for the exact amount of **$18,536.75**! Where would you like to receive your check?"

My wife and I rushed to the nearest Navy Federal location, grabbed the check, then rushed to City Hall. I walked up to the third floor and found the engineering office. I handed the engineer the check directly and asked "How soon can you start work?"

The road closure announcement happened the next day. The sewer lateral line was installed within a week.

Chapter 37
December 2018

The quick thinking on the sewer lateral line didn't save Christmas. Manius was quick to blame the city for missing his Christmas deadline, ignoring all the other missed deadlines and probably hoping I would unite behind a common enemy. He managed to give me this rough news while I was on travel for work in Poland. That spurned an angry response from me. I was tired of all the excuses. I was struggling for money, made worse by having to take a giant loan for a sewer line. I had finally snapped and left a particularly nasty voicemail on Manius' phone.

I regretted the voicemail the next day, and called back and apologized. Since I was traveling, I had Rachel handle more of the interactions with Manius, which helped buffer angry responses from both sides. At this point though, the relationship between myself and LuMa Construction was becoming increasingly hostile. I was fed up with them, and the temporary bright moments in construction could no longer cover for my bad feelings from the delays and surprise costs.

Late December meant cabinet installation. Inside, the house now had drywall, working plumbing and working electrical. It was being conditioned so that the drywall could be finished and no humidity would damage the inside. Granted, humidity isn't much of a factor in December, but conditioning the air in a house somehow transforms it from a construction project into a living space. I can't explain it, it's one of those things where you just have to be there to understand.

The cabinet company that Manius used gave us a great deal. Not only did they install beautiful cabinets, but they helped us select a beautiful granite for all the counter tops. Even the bathroom cabinets, which I frankly didn't care much about, looked really nice. Cabinets and counter tops are the kind of things you don't really appreciate until they are installed. Then, suddenly, the room just looks better and gains so much more functionality because of the cabinetry.

Cabinets also improved Rachel's mood. We drove to the house to do another walkthrough. As she walked through the kitchen, I could see her mentally placing all of our kitchen appliances into her dream kitchen that she had designed. It brought a smile to a face too often weary from apartment living and a pregnancy due in February.

December also brought a phone call from the moving company. They would no longer store our stuff starting in January. Since we didn't have a Certificate of Occupancy, or CO, I couldn't live in the house. However, I could move my stuff in. Manius agreed to shift work to finish the upstairs so that we could fit everything into the upstairs rooms while the downstairs was being finished. We set a date of 8 January for the move.

A moving date improved my mood, even if it only involved our stuff. My hope was maybe the house would be done by then and we could move in for real, but I knew that was a pipe dream.

Christmas came and passed. Rachel and I put up a small Christmas tree in our tiny apartment. It was, quite literally, the Charlie Brown Christmas Tree. The kids were really good sports about it. Incredibly, despite all the craziness they had been through, they continued to bounce back. Time and time again, I would be stressed that things weren't going as planned, and yet it would barely bother any of the kids. I sometimes wish I had their resiliency.

Christmas also made me think long and hard about money. I could now literally not afford any more mistakes. We had zero reserves left. My excellent credit score was going to take a pounding with the amount of debt I took on, and there was little I could do about it. The scary part was that if something else failed, I would have built ninety-five percent of a house only to have it all crash down at the end and fall apart. And if that happened, then what? I didn't have a backup plan. My credit would be hurt enough it would be hard to start fresh.

As a military officer, I always tried to have a backup plan. If something goes wrong, having a backup plan, even if it isn't perfect, gives you a quick strategy to shift to. It gives you that chance to immediately move out of danger and head in a direction, even if that direction isn't the best direction. In my case, I had no backup plan. I knew that building a house was expensive, but I hadn't thought I would be stuck in an apartment with the house six months overdue. I certainly didn't expect to pay for a sewer lateral line.

The future was a bit bleak. What if we had a baby in the apartment? What if the city came back and screwed us on something else? What if Manius had his own financial issues and suddenly went bankrupt? My mind raced through all sorts of circumstances. My friends would tell me "I've never heard of a home building story like yours," and my only thought was "I really hope it has a good ending."

Chapter 38

January 8 brought a rain scare in the morning, but only briefly. Our family drove to the house early to meet the movers. Cabinet work and drywall mudding were still ongoing, so we had carved out areas in the center of each room where our stuff could be placed. Luckily there was enough space for us to do this, since this house was larger than our previous homes, and the upstairs was essentially finished at this point.

The downside was that nothing could be assembled or unpacked. Military moves are unique in that the movers are paid to both pack up all your stuff as well as unpack and take the packing materials away. Many of my military friends elect to unpack themselves, but I don't like doing that. I've seen it take weeks to unpack all your items, put them away and become properly situated, and I just don't have that kind of time. Plus, when the movers unpack, it makes it easy to verify all of your items have arrived. Plus plus, if something is damaged, you can note it right there, which makes filing your claim easier. You technically have two years to file a moving claim for any damaged property, but in reality, if you don't finish it by your second month after a move, you'll probably forget and just live with the damages.

I've had terrible movers in the past. When we moved into a house in Suffolk, Virginia, the movers from "Two Men And a Truck" arrived in the middle of a rainstorm with no tarp covering our open boxes, which is supposed to be required before they leave their shop. The movers brought everything in with muddy boots and no ground covering, another missed requirement. I guess their company really was two men and a truck, and you'd have to pay extra for services requiring tarps or proper rain coverings. My wife opened one box that had her preserved wedding dress, which was now damaged due to the rain. At that point, seven months pregnant with our first child, she was pretty angry.

But the kicker for me was the mover's attempt to weasel their way out of unpacking. The head mover declared they were finished and asked me to sign the form. I asked why everything wasn't unpacked.

Mover: "We don't unpack items."

Me: "For military moves, that's a requirement."

Mover: "Well, that isn't for this form."

Me: Reading form. "It says below the signature line "Boxes unpacked and materials removed from premises."

Mover: "Well, we don't do that."

Me: "How about we talk to your manager."

Sure enough, manager on the phone told him to unpack items. The movers, really not happy at this point, began slinging items out of boxes. After about ten minutes, I told them to leave, and I returned their sarcastic replies with a string of obscenities that would make a crusty Sailor blush. Not my finest hour. I called their manager and laid into her, wondering why on earth I had deployed around the world to protect America when I got treated like garbage for simply insisting her movers do what the contract required.

To her credit, she sent out a whole new team the next day, who unpacked our items with care and removed all the packing materials. I followed up with an accurate review that balanced my initial experience with her efforts to fix the issue.

Thankfully, this moving company wasn't just two men and a truck. They had four particularly large guys and were extremely thorough with their documentation. They had brought plenty of coverings to protect our new flooring and carpet. They were very kind to my wife and kids, and understanding of our non-ideal circumstances. For what I hoped was our last military move, we had apparently lucked out.

While the moving people were nice, our stuff was not in great shape. The master bedroom set headboard was snapped in two places, rendering it completely useless, and the long vertical cracks meant I couldn't fix it. Our dining room set was beaten and abused. It looked as if someone had mindlessly tossed our dining room chairs into a storage container. Luckily, the set was made from heavy wood, so it had absorbed the abuse like a prize fighter, still standing while looking something awful.

The movers were apologetic. They had taken this move from another company, and didn't realize how poorly that company had boxed everything. Later in the year I would meet with the owner of the moving company, showing him pictures of the damage. He and I would settle for a fair amount of money. In the end, I got a new master bedroom set and mattress out of the deal, which was far better than many of my previous moving claims.

Moving day also brought more lousy news. Manius said the city was being stubborn about finishing the certificate of occupancy for the house. They would sign a temporary CO, but not a permanent one. Manius was fine with me moving into the upstairs with a temporary CO. I was not. The last thing I wanted was to move into our home and then be forced out by the city because Manius couldn't get the city to complete the CO paperwork.

The other concern was closing. The mortgage company was itching to close. They had extended the mortgage well past the point of normal construction to permit loans. They wanted it done, and they were withholding money from LuMa Construction until they finished. That put enormous pressure on Manius and Lucius to finish the project. I was OK with this enormous pressure, because while it seemed Manius didn't care much about my complaints, he perked up an awful lot when the mortgage company withheld thousands of dollars.

Moving in on a temporary CO was not going to happen. I would lose the financial incentive and pressure on LuMa Construction, and I would put myself at risk of eviction. I called the mortgage company and asked them to set 14 January as a closing date.

Chapter 39

W e moved into our home on a temporary CO. Because LuMa Construction had caught the eye of the Mayor of Chesapeake, the Deputy City Manager insisted that everything on the house be completed before issuing a full Certificate of Occupancy. This included the basic landscaping. While Facebook Messaging the Mayor had worked to solve the sewer line problem and receive a temporary CO, it hadn't made LuMa Construction particularly popular with the bureaucrats in the city government.

Yet another issue cropped up, this time concerning the drainage ditch. In front of our home was a ditch, with a driveway going over a culvert. The culvert was old, but it worked just fine. The city told Manius he would have to move the culvert closer to the house, because they wanted to be able to expand the road. This didn't make any sense for two reasons. One, the electrical lines were on my side of the road, and normally you move the road on the side without electrical so you don't have to move really tall poles. Second, all the culverts on the other side of the road were offset from the street. This was likely done to expand the street in that direction, not towards my house.

Manius fought this change, and despite my anger at him, I felt sorry about the situation. The city was being a pain in the butt over yet another thing. None of the city engineers had brought up the culvert until now. Where were these idiots in 2018? Who knows! Certainly not checking the sewer connection, and certainly not paying enough attention to our site plan. Luckily for us, after a bit of a Mexican standoff, the City of Chesapeake backed down on the issue of moving the culvert.

In the meantime, I was getting desperate. I called Vance and Tatiana from the mortgage company to express my concerns. I did not want to run out of cash, but I simply couldn't afford to keep sitting in The Amber apartment. I also couldn't let LuMa Construction off the hook or our house would never be completed. Vance and Tatiana agreed, so they agreed to close on the house but withhold a final payment until the full Certificate of Occupancy came in from the city. This would get me out of hot water while holding enough money from LuMa Construction that they would maintain motivation to finish.

I didn't particularly enjoy doing this, but I didn't have a choice. I don't like withholding payment from people for work, and I really hate paying people late. I prefer to take people at their word, and I'm a patient person. But I was desperate. The Amber was clamoring for another one-month extension, and we couldn't wait any longer.

Luckily, moving out of our apartment was easy. We didn't have much stuff, and it only took two trips to empty the apartment. By this point, the upstairs was essentially done, so it was really only the cabinets, some minor electrical work, and the drywall and painting that had to be finished. The only downside was that we couldn't hang anything on the walls, or put any furniture next to the walls.

I was overjoyed to leave The Amber. The winter had brought cold enough weather that it forced people inside. Between the weather and staying on top of the outside smokers, it had been somewhat peaceful the past month. I knew that would change the minute it warmed up, and I was tired of fighting people on basic things, like not blaring their music or screaming bloody murder at each other at two in the morning. Sure, we would have to deal with workers in our living space, but that was a far cry from our neighbors in the apartment.

The kids were excited to have real rooms. Sure, they had to essentially live-in makeshift furniture huts in the middle of the room, and they couldn't decorate how they wanted, but it beat apartment living. They also had a backyard, of sorts anyway. Our property was heavily wooded, and the grass really wasn't growing anywhere near the house. In fact, it was kind of a muddy, murky swamp around us. My kids wanted to explore though, so we planned our first journey into the backyard.

My youngest child, Rosalynn, wanted to explore the vast expanse of our property. It had rained the previous day, so we donned boots and traipsed into the backyard. Multiple times I had to save Rosalynn from sucking, nasty mud that threatened to pull her into the abyss. But Rosalynn, ever resilient, continued onwards until we finally reached the back of our property, where we turned around and made a beeline for the house.

That's when it all went wrong. Rosalynn got tangled up in the undergrowth and tried to pull herself out, grabbing onto a vine. We would later learn the vine was called a greenbrier. Wikipedia has a note about the greenbrier, saying "The thorny thickets can effectively protect small animals from larger predators who cannot enter the prickly tangle." Add "human beings" to the list of larger predators that shouldn't enter the prickly tangle. Rosalynn let out a piercing scream as the greenbrier thorns penetrated her small hands. I made my way over as quickly as possible and carried her out of the woods, getting scratched by the same plants in the process.

Once I finished patching up her hands and wiping away the tears, Rosalynn seemed to be in a better place. After a small snack, she asked for some paper to draw on. I walked by to see her furiously drawing a picture. Curious, I crept up and spied over her shoulder. On the paper was a drawing of a little girl with a talking "bubble" that said "I hate thorns." Next to her were a bunch of crudely drawn thorn plants, each with their own talking bubbles. "We hate you too," "Go Away" and "You're ugly" were the thorns' response to Rosalynn's two-dimensional self-portrait.

I burst out laughing. Rosalynn could be a sweet girl, but when she got angry, she could be absolutely savage.

Chapter 40

February 8, 2019

I began this book with a birth, so it seems appropriate to end it on that same note. Rachel had on again, off again contractions in February, and by the morning of the 8th, it was obvious that the baby was going to arrive. We arrived at Portsmouth Naval Hospital early in the morning and after an epidural and a bit of Pitocin, baby Felix arrived. He was...really big. Like, over ten pounds big. Bigger than pretty much every other baby in the hospital. I joked that he was big enough to beat up the neighboring babies and take their milk money. It brought a laugh from most of the nurses and Rachel, so it was a big win for a little dad joke.

Baby Felix came home a few days later. Rachel and I found it odd that our house will be the only one he will grow up in. Our previous kids had lived in Virginia, Hawaii, Connecticut and Georgia at various times in their lives, in different homes and in different circumstances. Not Felix. He would grow up in one home, in a completely different lifestyle. For many people, moving once is a traumatic experience, but for my family, it was the normal. Now, suddenly, our normal was different.

My parents came down to help with Baby Felix for a week while I took a short trip to Estonia. My job was demanding more time, and I couldn't postpone the trip. Later that year I would spend almost a month aboard the *USS MOUNT WHITNEY* in the Baltic Sea, deeply involved in a large, multi-national exercise with many of our European allies.

Our home saga wasn't finished until January of 2020. The company Manius used to mud the drywall had done a terrible job, and I noticed it days before the painters were due to arrive. I pointed it out, figuring it would be easy to fix it now before painting happened. The drywall mudder came back and somehow did a worse job, not just with the walls, but he also managed to sling drywall mud on our stuff in the center of each room.

After the painters left, we noticed that the paint literally flaked off the wall like dust. Manius assured us this was normal. After a bit of Google searching, I figured out that the drywall guy had never sanded the walls smooth. The proper way to install drywall is to screw in the large sheets of drywall, put up drywall tape (which has a grid pattern on it) over the seams, spread drywall mud (with a consistency similar to plaster) over the tape and then sand it all smooth. The primer and paint will easily soak into drywall, but if it isn't sanded, it sits on top and flakes off.

Had Manius insisted on fixing the drywall previously, the house saga would have been complete. I wasn't upset at him when I initially caught the issue. Contractors make mistakes, it's just something that happens. I was angry that he refused to fix the issue before painting, and then when it was obviously messed up, he refused to admit the mistake.

It came to a head in November 2019, when I had a home inspector note the paint as "poor workmanship." That is a trigger phrase for the Department of Veteran's Affairs to pursue legal action against a builder. Manius knew that too. Suddenly we were in discussion on how to fix it. He did eventually pay for painters to come out, sand the walls and fix everything. Well, almost everything. To this day I'm finding areas, like the back of a closet, that they missed. Someday I'll have extra money and time to properly sand the walls smooth and paint them.

Our final landscaping was a mixed bag. Lucius had done a great job raising our house up with loads of sand and dirt. That was important because it let the water from a hard rain drain away quickly. We noticed that while many of our neighbors had flooded yards after a day of rain, all of our water drained into the ditch. But the landscaping portion was terrible. Lucius simply spread cheap grass seed on the sandy, clay mix of soil that obviously lacked the nutrients needed to grow real grass. It took nearly a year before there was enough grass to make the yard not a muddy disaster. I would eventually bring in a few yards of a topsoil/compost mix and new grass seed to grow an actual yard.

During the summer and fall I cut a path through our woods. The greenbriers that had stuck Rosalynn in the hand fell before a sharpened machete, weed whacker and set of clippers. After carving a path, I poured wood chips onto the path to level it out and make it easy to walk on. I found a website, chipdrop.com, that partnered with local arborist companies to find people willing to take wood chips. Most companies would pay a lot of money to dispose of wood chips at the local dump, but I was willing to take them for free.

By December of 2019, the house was essentially complete. I had fought and won our battle to have the walls sanded and properly painted. Our landscaping was slowly coming along, and the woods was now regularly traveled by my children. On one of the coldest days of the month, we lit a roaring fire in our fire place that radiated heat all throughout our home. Well into the night, after everyone but me had gone to bed, I sat there by the fireplace, staring into the coals. The glowing coals returned my stare with a sort of primordial energy. I drifted off a bit, pondering how over the centuries of human existence, from the time we lived in caves to now, we still find it normal to gather around a fire, and to build our homes around a heat source. It's not uncommon to have a fireplace as the centerpiece of a room, and whether it's lit by wood, coal, or gas, the flickering flames of the fire draw us in with an almost magical attraction.

I pondered how, years earlier, I had started my quest to build a house. From dreaming about it, designing it, and then suffering through the challenges of building it, I had come out on top. I had built a house, from scratch, on a piece of land that not long ago was covered in trees. Staring into that fire, thinking about how not long before this same spot was simply a patch of dirt in the woods made me smile at my accomplishment.

But I knew it was far from over. Sure, I had built a house. But it wasn't yet a home. Much work remained to be done to truly tame the outdoors and indoors, to become real neighbors and a real part of our community. Plus, with a large house, I needed a family routine to maintain it. Yes, we would start the year 2020 with a house. But what we really needed to do was build a home.

Epilogue

Whenever anyone listens to my house building saga, typically while enjoying an adult beverage, the first question normally asked is "Would you do it all over again?" My answer has always been "Yes." I once thought long and hard about that answer, because at various points I really questioned the wisdom of building the house, our choice of builder, the whole process and the build timing. But when I look back at it, I can't discern what I could have done differently. I had saved a lot of money. I had come to the table with a home design. I didn't make last minute changes. I did interview a lot of home builders. I certainly didn't have rose-tinted glasses on when I made the decisions that I did.

When people are surprised by that answer, I always ask what they think I could have done differently. Some say they would have fired LuMa Construction in the middle of the project. That sounds splendid on paper, but in reality, you'd be stuck with a half-finished house. What construction company would want to pick up the pieces? Would that company provide a warranty for their work? Do you have the cash just sitting around to do it yourself? Plus, finding a new construction company takes time and research. Does your job give you the flexibility to take this time off?

The cold, hard reality is that once you pick a builder and start building, short of them going out of business or committing a crime, you're stuck with them. If you're super rich, you can afford to hire and fire people at will, but I, like most people, had to build on a very real budget with very inflexible finances. And let's face it, if you're super rich, you'll just chill out in your super rich apartment, not dealing with loud people consuming illegal drugs and threatening to harm others at two in the morning.

Some people tell me I could have waited. That list of people includes my wife, who on at least two occasions was quite willing to throw in the towel and delay building our forever home. "We can just buy a place and then re-attack later" she told me at one point. I won't lie, it was tempting at times to take that option and make the pain go away. But I have a saying about waiting, which is "The best time to start a project was in the past. The next best time is now." You can spend plenty of time second-guessing whether "now" is the right time, and to be fair, sometimes "now" is not the right time. But waiting isn't always better, and all things being equal, it's better to start a project than to wait.

In this case, the future came out on my side. In March 2020 the United States essentially shut down in response to the COVID-19 pandemic. The U.S. government responded by lowering interest rates, which caused a massive boom in building. Lumber went out of stock and prices more than tripled. Home prices also skyrocketed, and builders couldn't build fast enough. Had we waited even a year to build, we might have been stuck with a half-finished house in the middle of a pandemic, or trying to build a house with lumber over twice the cost of normal. It is highly likely that we wouldn't have built a home, and we would have spent more time in a house that wasn't our "forever home."

Another common response to my saga is "you should have done more research." I had two motivations for writing this book: illuminating the custom home building process, and memorializing the home that Rebecca was supposed to grow up in. I haven't yet found a single person that built a home the way I did. Nobody did it from scratch. Nobody did it on the sort of budget I had. And certainly nobody had the nasty challenges I did, which left me unable to believe anyone's promises at face value. Yet I came to the table understanding as much of the construction process as any normal person might. I had built things before. I am pretty mechanically inclined, and when I didn't understand something, I did plenty of research. For crying out loud, I geeked out about "encapsulated crawl spaces." What normal person does that? The truth is, I couldn't have been more prepared understanding the home building process.

My next most common question is "Was it worth it," and my answer is again "Yes." I love my house. I love that my house is setup how I wanted it. I designed it. I have my office. I have my kegerator. I have a beautiful fireplace. My wife has her own space with its bright windows and nice cabinets. I love that the bathroom in our mudroom makes it easy to enjoy the outdoors without dragging mud throughout the house. I love our covered porch that is enjoyable even when its hot outside. These furnishings just don't exist in a builder-grade house that someone else designed.

Some people ask if I've forgiven Manius and Lucius. Sadly, we didn't part on great terms. After a particularly negative online exchange, Lucius called me a coward in a rather nasty email. I haven't talked to him since then. The last time I talked to Manius was in January 2020.

I would say I've come to terms with LuMa Construction. I'm still angry over the whole experience. In my opinion, Manius took on a massive project that was a bit bigger than he expected. He probably assumed that there would be no issues, which any project manager will tell you is a terrible assumption to make. Had Manius started earlier, he could have finished on-time, and we'd probably be on better terms. I never sued him or his company over any of the events documented here. I removed my negative online reviews and never submitted a negative VA review, despite my anger over the situation, and despite the facts being in my favor to do so. I didn't use their real names in this book, despite all the information on these events being accurate and documented.

Is that forgiveness? Maybe. I'll let you be the judge.

My house may be complete, but my home is not. Sitting in the garage is a plywood box with Rebecca's headstone in it. The new cemetery we re-interred her at only allowed bronze plates. I have carved out an area on our property to erect a small chapel, where I plan to place the headstone. It'll be an area to retreat from the world for some small peace. It's part of my plan to build a nice homestead that my family can enjoy for the years to come. While building a house was a challenge, it was never the final goal. The final goal was always to build a home.

Appendix: The long list of lessons learned

Many people likely read this book to learn how to build a custom house and avoid the pitfalls I encountered along the way. To make that easy, I've captured these in a sort of chronological order in this appendix to help you.

BEFORE YOU BUILD

- Write out requirements. I cannot stress this enough, it's probably the most important thing you will do. You need a sheet of paper with exactly what you want your future house to do for you. This goes well beyond wall colors and granite pattern. To start, ask the following questions:

1. How many people will live there 5, 10 and 20 years from now? Be sure to account for future babies and aging parents.

2. What is the worst weather your area gets, and how will you deal with it? How do you deal with emergencies like earthquakes, hurricanes and floods?

3. What work do you perform in the house? Do you cook at home? Work in a home office?

4. Do children play in your home? If so, where will they play? Will they play outside? Will they bring their friends over? Do you need a place that is quiet?

5. How many people come to visit you? How long do they stay? Do they eat dinner, or just stop by for coffee?

6. For the people living in the house, what is

their daily routine? When do they wake up, use the bathroom, eat, wash their clothes, and go to bed? Where and how much storage do they need?

These questions will help you tease out what you need a house to do for you. For example, if your area floods, you need a house that resists flooding, so you might spend more on an encapsulated crawl space and grading. Someone who loves to entertain and cook may want a larger kitchen island that will hold more food for guests. It's important to write this out on a sheet of paper and list it in priority order. That way, if you have to compromise, you can properly weigh your options.

- Build a list of videos, websites, and articles that you find related to your build. It'll help you when you later think "I remember watching this video talk about foundations, but now I can't find it!"

- Do tons of research, but take everything with a grain of salt. Many ways of building homes are now old or antiquated, and sometimes you have to dig to find new information. For example, most of the articles on pressure treated wood still reference wood treated with chromated arsenicals, despite the fact this wood has been banned since 2004.

- Save up money. Put money into a high-interest savings account, or buy a stablecoin cryptocurrency and put it in an interest-bearing account. Save up more than you think you need. Remember there is no such thing as a "no money down" custom built home.

RESEARCHING YOUR SITE

- Go back to your requirements list and consider how your home's location affects your requirements. If you like to cook at home, how far away is the grocery store? What about your favorite places to eat? Schools? Hospital? When something is over thirty minutes away, it's not a "quick trip." Maybe that doesn't bother you now, but if it takes over an hour round trip to run basic errands, you might feel a bit isolated.

- Do you want neighbors? Some people love neighbors, others love complete privacy, and then there is everyone else in the middle. When you're reviewing a site, try to visit the site at different times of day. Is it quiet at night, or is everyone partying, and what are you OK with?

- Where do water, sewer, internet, gas, cable and electrical lines enter your property? Don't trust a builder to tell you, call the city to verify where utilities are located. Get that in writing. Utilities, especially in an area that is being developed, have a huge impact on the price of your home and the land it's on. Fighting the city over utilities is almost always a losing proposition unless they explicitly promised them to you.

- Think about shade and sun. You don't want trees hanging over your house, but shade on your house will buffer wind, rain and heat. The builder will have you stake the four corners of the house and will take out whatever trees you want gone. Think that through. Are you going to install solar? You might want a clear roof then. What about setting up a kid's playground? It's easier to cut huge trees when there isn't the risk of hitting a home, so having an idea of your future lawn setup can save you time and money later. Pay particular attention to where the sun rises and sets, and what parts of your house and yard are shaded at each time of day.

- Lookup property taxes, zoning and school zones. Read the local news station websites and talk to future neighbors. Did electrical rates rise? Is a new toll bridge being planned down the road? Did the city just pass a locality tax rate? Will the schools get rezoned? Most cities have a twenty-year plan, which outlines what the city zoning and major roads will look like in the future. Read this plan, lest your quiet home become suddenly located on a busy street.

- Build a spreadsheet to compare living costs. If you're considering living in different counties, cities or states, the daily cost of living can be dramatically different. Factor in driving costs, state and local taxes, school costs and the average grocery and eating out bill. For example, many people encouraged me to live in nearby Suffolk, since I could purchase a home for slightly cheaper. When I did the calculation, I realized that over the long term, the gas and toll costs would negate any benefits of living out that far.

DESIGNING YOUR HOME

- Start with requirements and a square. Draw a big square and place the rooms where you want them to intersect each other. If you want a two-story house, do this for downstairs and upstairs. Once you have the basic layout, start to size your rooms. Be sure to note specific features, like fireplaces, that you want.

- Open concept equals radiated noise. Especially if you have kids or parties, if there are no walls to absorb the noise, then it will be loud. Consider having rooms insulated for noise if you need quiet in a particular place.

- I recommend using an architect or home designer that you can meet with. Yes, you can go online, but meeting with someone gives you a chance to ask questions and have that conversation on your home. Also, local people have worked with the local government and probably understand what will and won't survive contact with your city government's inspectors.

- Look at the cost per square foot in the area you are building. That will likely be about what it costs to build your home. At the very least, this is a starting point when you discuss prices.

- Remember that the home design is king, because it becomes what the city inspector uses. If you put a pull-down ironing board in there, and the builder forgets to install it, it's easy to require them to do so. Verbal agreements to modify a plan should always be captured in writing.

- Don't forget the outside! Do you want a hot tub later in life? In-ground irrigation for your lawn? Factor those into your home design. Having the electrical and plumbing that supports these items, even if you don't install them right away, saves you money in the long term.

INTERVIEWING YOUR TEAM

- Custom builders vary widely, from the small part-time builder to large companies. The most important things are price, schedule and how comfortable you are with them. If someone laughs at your design and says it's stupid, their price doesn't matter, because it's not going to be a pleasant experience and you should find someone else. Find a builder that can stay inside your budget and timeline, and is OK with your home design.

- Builders have mortgage companies they like to use and vice versa. It's normally best to stick with what a builder uses unless you have a compelling reason to deviate. If your builder and mortgage company haven't worked together before, make darn sure they quickly develop a working relationship.

- Ask to see a builder's previous work. If you can, talk to a homeowner they built a home for a year or two earlier.

- See if the builder will hire a landscaping firm for the final landscaping. Landscaping is a particular weak spot for custom builders. It may be better to spend a bit more for a professional company than accept builder grade grass that you'll have to change later.

SIGNING THE CONTRACTS

- The build contract is gold. Whatever is written in there is what gets enforced. If legal issues happen, then everyone will clam up and execute exactly per contract unless you specifically let them out of it. So, if you want something specific, it better be in the contract. Want the builder to pay for cost overruns? If it's not in the contract, it's not happening.

- Similarly, once you submit the approved home design and plan, the builder can charge for change orders. I recommend using a PowerPoint with room-by-room descriptions of what you want, and go over those with your builder. Give him a copy. Don't make him guess on anything. If you want white trim, purple walls and golden door handles, you better give him the shade of paint for each with a brand name and number. More details are better, as it helps prevent confusion when there are subcontractors trying to build your home quickly.

- Find the city or county website that tracks building permits and track your permit. If the builder says "everything is fine," but you don't see permit approval, everything is not fine.

- Discuss how you want to be updated by the builder. Once a week is normally good enough for much of the build. Daily may be better when you reach the point of electrical and plumbing installation and are close to closing.

- Ask about screws and nails. It is better for drywall and decks to be screwed instead of nailed. It does take a bit longer, and may cost more, but if you can afford it, screws save you the headache of nail pops later on.

DURING THE BUILD

- Visit the site when you're able, and let your builder know when you're coming. Yes, it's your home, but maybe that day is bad because the inspector is there. Surprising your builder with a visit isn't a smart move. Besides, most builders want homeowners on site so they can be assured the new home meets expectations.

- Stay on top of loan draws. Pay your interest-only mortgage payment on time. Finances can bring everything to a screeching halt.

- Don't be afraid to verify the builder has performed all the work before approving a draw. Builders can get ahead of themselves, but if you approve a draw and there is unfinished work, you could be left holding the bag.

- Hesitate to make large changes. Paint and even flooring is easy to change early on. Adding a room requires an updated permit and can significantly delay construction. Document all changes in writing, and ensure the cost is captured as well.

- Video or photograph walls before they close them with drywall. That helps if you ever have to renovate in the future.

AS YOU GET CLOSE TO THE END

- Keep track of final inspections and the Certificate of Occupancy. You aren't closing on a mortgage without them.

- If you close with unfinished work, you'll receive a "punch list" of items for the builder to complete. Make sure you verify each one.

- Do a walkthrough with your builder. Be really thorough. Flush every toilet, turn on every sink and light, open every door and window. Take a copy of the home design with you and verify everything is where it's supposed to be.

MOVING DAY

- Remember that new homes lack furnishings. Curtains are an item that you may want to install before moving day, unless you like exposing yourself to your neighbors.

- Meet your neighbors. Its super easy to knock on a door, introduce yourself and say that you just moved in. That breaks the ice early and jump starts relationships.

- Take a house walkthrough video before moving in. It'll be the last time the house is empty.

AFTER MOVE-IN

- Understand your warranty terms. Most builders honor a one-year warranty on pretty much everything in the house.

- Doors and windows move out of alignment as a house settles on the foundation. Have the builder adjust any sticky doors or windows after six months. Make sure they adjust the hinge first! Too often they want to sand the door down, but don't let them do that.

- Schedule a home inspection at around the ten-month point. This will give you an independent inspection and enough time to have the builder fix any other issues before your warranty expires.

- Be sure to submit the warranty cards on everything in the house. This includes: water heater, air conditioning or heat pumps, air handling units, roof shingles, stove, dishwasher, refrigerator, your fixtures (sinks, faucets, handles, etc.), fans, specialty lights, washer and dryer, doors, windows, dehumidifiers, circuit breakers and garage doors, to name just a few. Many companies provide better warranties if you register early.

- Have the builder provide the information of the company that sprayed your home for termites, and schedule future re-spraying with them. Termite sprays have fairly standard pricing, but you have a higher chance of getting a discount from the company that initially sprayed your home.

- Watch your city government's first home assessment. If the price is significantly higher or lower, you want to contest it right away. Remember that the city assessment is used for tax purposes, so if it's a bit low, that works in your favor.

- Check the plans that the city has on file for the house. Too often these are wrong. This causes an issue later if you refinance your mortgage and a lazy assessor looks at the city diagram rather than actually walking around your house to assess value. Not that I would ever have encountered that problem before...

Acknowledgement

While I did in fact write this book myself, there are many people that helped me turn my words into a page-turning reality.

First, I want to thank the many people that read draft copies of this book and provided useful editing advice: Jason Moser, Victor Spears, Lou Shearer and Jim Osborn. It's not easy to read someone's 57,000+ words in your "copious" amount of free time and then write recommendations. Gentlemen, I truly appreciate the time you took to help make this book flow so much better than my first draft.

Second, my cover designer, Shalone Cason, deserves a lot of credit. Shalone is a fellow Catholic that I first met while trying to fix our Church's crappy internet, and ever since then I keep discovering how talented he is in areas I am not talented at all. Shalone created the cover for this book and really helped me with branding, keywords and marketing. Anyone who has sold books knows that its too easy to get lost in the myriad of online books, and Shalone really helped me set this book apart from the competition.

Finally, I would be remiss if I didn't acknowledge the love and support from my family. I wrote this book during a hard time in my life. Shortly after my house was truly complete and I began seriously working on this book, the COVID-19 pandemic turned my whole world upside down, making my home and work life pretty challenging. There were quite a few days I struggled to just get up and get moving forward. The loving support from my wife, Rachel, and my kids gave me the focus I needed to keep working through the challenges. I couldn't wish for a better family.

About The Author

Ryan Haag

Ryan has spent much of his life building. Whether its building programs and teams of people in the Navy, or building a kids playplace in his backyard, Ryan enjoys the process of building order out of otherwise chaos. When he's not busy building something or writing, Ryan enjoys sipping on his home brewed beer and taking relaxing walks in the forest on his homestead in southeastern Virginia.

Made in the USA
Middletown, DE
26 August 2021